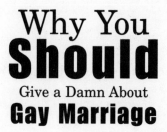

Why You
Should
Give a Damn About
Gay Marriage

Why You
Should
Give a Damn About
Gay Marriage

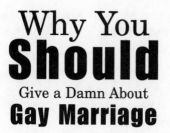

By Davina Kotulski, Ph.D.

Advocate
BOOKS

A NOTE TO READERS

THIS BOOK IS IN NO WAY MEANT TO BE A SUBSTITUTE FOR LEGAL ADVICE AND SOME FACTS MAY NOT BE COMPLETELY ACCURATE AT TIME OF PUBLICATION. PLEASE CONSULT AN ATTORNEY, GAY & LESBIAN ADVOCATES AND DEFENDERS (GLAD), LAMBDA LEGAL, OR THE NATIONAL CENTER FOR LESBIAN RIGHTS FOR MORE COMPLETE INFORMATION ABOUT THE LAWS IN YOUR AREA.

MANUFACTURED IN THE UNITED STATES OF AMERICA.

THIS TRADE PAPERBACK ORIGINAL IS PUBLISHED BY ADVOCATE BOOKS,
AN IMPRINT OF ALYSON PUBLICATIONS,
P.O. BOX 4371, LOS ANGELES, CALIFORNIA 90078-4371.
DISTRIBUTION IN THE UNITED KINGDOM BY TURNAROUND PUBLISHER SERVICES LTD.,
UNIT 3, OLYMPIA TRADING ESTATE, COBURG ROAD, WOOD GREEN,
LONDON N22 6TZ ENGLAND.

FIRST EDITION: APRIL 2004

04 05 06 07 08 ✳ 10 9 8 7 6 5 4 3 2

ISBN: 1-55583-873-1

CREDITS
• ART DIRECTION BY MATT SAMS
• COVER DESIGN BY VALERIE WAGNER.
• BACK COVER PHOTO OF AUTHOR BY CHLOE ATKINS.
• "AN OVERVIEW OF WHAT AB 205 WILL AND WON'T DO (WITH COMPARISONS TO CIVIL MARRIAGE," © JON W. DAVIDSON, REPRODUCED BY PERMISSION.
• SECTIONS FROM "LEFT AT THE ALTAR," © NATIONAL CENTER FOR LESBIAN RIGHTS, REPRODUCED BY PERMISSION.

To the love of my life, Molly McKay

Contents

Introduction

How I Became
a Marriage
Activist

When Molly McKay and I met in a country-and-western bar and realized we shared (among other things) a fondness for karaoke and Muppet movies, there was no doubt in our minds that we would marry.

My first foray into marriage activism started when Molly and I set a date for our wedding and were thrust into explaining ourselves to the jeweler, the baker, our parents, the owner of the place where we wanted to get married, and several other questioning individuals. It was an entirely new coming-out process. Three months before our marriage we decided to go to the 1998 San Francisco Pride Parade in full wedding attire. Molly wore a vintage bridal dress and drove her motorcycle, while I wore a tux, rode on the back, and carried a sign that read SUPPORT SAME-SEX MARRIAGE. The next morning our picture showed up on the cover of a major San Francisco newspaper.

We realized that one or two people really can make a difference. The outpouring of congratulations we received was inspiring. This was the first time either of us had received overwhelming social approval for being in a same-sex relationship, and it was incredible. It made me comprehend the kind of experience heterosexuals have on their wedding days and throughout their lives— and how vastly different it feels to be gay or lesbian. From that moment on Molly and I committed ourselves to making our marriage legal.

Back then I understood the emotional and social inequities faced by same-sex couples, but I had no idea the extent to which we were being unfairly treated under the law. As my knowledge grew, so did my conviction. I became involved in the Hawaii Marriage Project, worked on the campaign to stop the Defense of Marriage Act in California, helped Californians for Same-Sex Marriage collect signatures to get a marriage bill on the ballot, and joined the board of Marriage Equality California to get the message out.

When I was offered the opportunity to write a book about why same-sex couples deserved the right to marry, I was thrilled. What a unique chance to help people understand this issue!

I can only hope that this book will spark conversations on buses and heated debate at dinner tables; that it will educate our own community as to why the right to legal civil marriage matters to us; and that it will persuade every fair-minded American, regardless of sexual orientation, why this is not a special rights issue—but a civil rights issue.

one

Silly Rabbit,
Marriage Is For
Heterosexuals!

Well, maybe not! There are more than 1,138* federal rights that accompany civil marriage, and some additional 300 per individual state. That means your run-of-the-mill marriage-license-carrying heterosexual couple has access to approximately 1,400 rights, benefits, and protections. I can repeat that again if you are still in shock: 1,400 rights, benefits, and protections. 1,400 is a big number. Just try and name 1,400 of your favorite songs or 1,400 of your closest friends.

Most of us don't even consider these rights until something goes horribly wrong, such as, for example, when Dick and John Doe travel to Florida to attend the summer White Party. After a few too many drinks, John slips on the dance floor and knocks himself unconscious. The ambulance comes to take John to the hospital, but because the two are considered legal strangers, Dick is not allowed to ride along. Dick hails a cab and rushes to keep up with the paramedics.

John is admitted to the emergency room, but the admitting nurse stops Dick at the door. When he explains their relationship, she looks at him with sympathetic eyes and,

---

*A 1996 General Accounting Office report found there were approximately 1,049 federal rights provided with civil marriage. In 2004 another report found that 89 new provisions had been added since 1996, increasing the total number of federal rights that accompany civil marriage to 1,138.

3

with a touch of Southern drawl, tells him that only next of kin are allowed in the emergency room. "We don't recognize those kinds of relationships here in Florida."

Of course, some people think gay people don't need marriage licenses. We just need good lawyers to draw up power of attorney contracts and medical directives to address these types of mishaps. But even the most neurotic of us don't always remember to keep copies of these documents in our luggage, let alone in our fanny packs. And what if your luggage gets shipped off to Seattle when you and your domestic partner are bound for Kentucky? Like that never happens!

In Dick and John's situation the important documents are filed away in a sock drawer in San Francisco, utterly useless in their time of need. Dick can't prove the documents exist and is thus unable to make medical decisions for John. Dick must begin the harrowing task of locating John's family to make sure John's wishes are carried out.

Gays and lesbians often come face-to-face with heterosexual privilege and the everyday perks it provides: A gay man waiting at the rental car check-out notices he's paying extra to put his partner down as a second driver, while the heterosexual couple next to him only pays for one because spouses have an automatic driving privilege. A lesbian couple's joint checking account statement shows two separate charges to their local gym because they don't qualify for a family membership.

"Marriage laws and rules weave a much more delicate and invisible web than most of us know. 'Married' is a shorthand taken seriously by banks, insurers, courts, employers, schools, hospitals, cemeteries, rental car companies, frequent flyer programs, and more."
—E.J. Graff, author of *What Is Marriage For?*

THE MARRIAGE DISCOUNT!

Every six months or so, I like to call my auto insurance company and ask them why I don't get the $360 per year "marriage discount" on my auto insurance. (If our marriage was recognized by the state, we'd have already saved an extra $1,800 plus interest in the past five years since our ceremony.) The customer service agent assures me that they are actually quite progressive for even allowing my domestic partner to be on my policy.

"Well, what are the guidelines for offering the marriage discount?" I persist. "What demographic data and factors contribute to making someone a good driver vis-à-vis marriage? Can I get a copy of them? Maybe we—"

"I'm sorry," the agent interrupts. "But we can't share those guidelines."

After some continued discussion, the entrapped agent—by then exasperated—agrees that it's crazy to offer marriage discounts to people who've been married for less than a week, while withholding it from longtime couples like Molly and me, who fit every definition of the word.

I don't know about *you all*, but I've been hit numerous times—by married people.

According to my customer service agent, it's not corporate greed, but the insurance commissioner who keeps the company from supporting our cause. State insurance commissioners establish the standards for rates; they establish premium guidelines based on research concerning what factors correlate with the probabilities of causing or being involved in an accident. LGBT couples are denied the "marriage discount" because there is no research indicating that being in a registered domestic partnership (or any other type of long-term committed same-sex relationship) reduces collision probability.

Why? Because no one is doing this research!

For the most part, these financial disparities—as with the bulk of our withheld rights—go by unnoticed. We are unaware of the extra taxes we pay, the discounts we don't get on our car insurance, and all the extra red tape we go through all because we can't legally marry.

Sure, the institution of marriage can be sexist and patri-archal, but that's the tradition of heterosexual marriage! Why does our version have to be? Are gay men suddenly going to start demanding that one or the other of them stay home, give up his career, and raise their children? Certainly there are no cultural norms dictating that a gay man's place is in the home. Would access to these 1,400 rights and responsibilities cause gay people to suddenly become overwhelmed by the expectations implicit in the phrase: to love and cherish in sickness and in health? Excuse me, but I thought we were already doing this with-out any help from society—and doing it pretty well.

If I have your attention, read on. Hatemongers—or what activist Owen Wolf likes to call "the religious reich"—keep throwing around the term *homosexual agen-da*. Now, let's talk about *their* agenda. Most of us, gay and straight, don't even know what the heck those 1,400 rights are, and the religious reich's agenda—*the anti-equality agenda*—is to keep it that way. In this book, you will learn the myriad of rights, responsibilities, and protections that come with civil marriage and the compelling reasons why gays and lesbians—whether single, cohabitating, divorced, widowed, joined in a domestic partnership or civil union, or married in a country more progressive than our own (such as Canada)—need to pursue full marriage equality in the United States.

Note: When referring to gay marriage, this book also intends to include a marriage in which one or both partners are transsexual. Because the law views transsexual status in conflicting ways, depending on the state of residence or the state of the person's transition, winning marriage equality for same-sex couples would allow transsexuals to marry whomever they chose, regardless of their own or their partner's gender identity. To the transsexual reader, I apologize for using "same-sex marriage," "gay marriage," and "marriage equality" interchangeably. I hope that you will understand my intent to include transsexuals' issues.

two

Test Your
Marriage IQ

Test your knowledge with this handy quiz!

1) How many rights currently come with a registered California domestic partnership?
   a. 15
   b. 50
   c. 200-300
   d. 1,000
   e. 1,138+

2) How many rights come with a Vermont civil union?
   a. 15
   b. 50
   c. 200-300
   d. 1,000
   e. 1,138+

3) How many rights come with a civil marriage license?
   a. 15
   b. 50
   c. 200-300
   d. 1,000
   e. 1,138+

4) In which countries were same-sex couples able to legally marry as of 2003?
   a. Canada, Australia, and the United States
   b. Canada, Austria, and New Zealand
   c. Canada, Belgium, and the Netherlands
   d. Canada, Belgium, and France
   e. Canada, France, and South Africa

5) In which states can same-sex couples be legally
   married?
   a. Hawaii, Vermont, and Rhode Island
   b. Hawaii, Vermont, and California
   c. Hawaii and Vermont
   d. Hawaii only
   e. None of the Above

6) While marriage is recognized in all 50 states, in what
   states are Vermont civil unions recognized?
   a. All 50 states
   b. Vermont, California, Hawaii, and Massachusetts
   c. Vermont, New Hampshire, New Jersey, and New
      York
   d. Vermont only
   e. Vermont and New York only

7) Which states recognize California domestic
   partnerships?
   a. All 50 states
   b. Vermont, California, Hawaii, and Massachusetts
   c. Vermont, New Hampshire, New Jersey, and New
      York
   d. California, Oregon, and Washington
   e. California only

8) Which states have had same-sex marriage lawsuits or currently have a case pending?
   a. Alaska, Hawaii, Massachusetts, New Jersey, and Vermont
   b. Alaska, Georgia, Nebraska, and South Dakota
   c. Kentucky, Minnesota, New York, Washington, and Wisconsin
   d. Arizona, California, Colorado, Florida, and Indiana
   e. Alaska, Arizona, California, Colorado, District of Columbia, Florida, Georgia, Hawaii, Indiana, Kentucky, Massachusetts, Minnesota, Nebraska, New Jersey, New York, Ohio, Pennsylvania, Vermont, Washington, and Wisconsin

Correct answers 1=a, 2=c, 3=e, 4=c, 5=e, 6=d, 7=e, 8=e

three

Rights Your
Average Incarcerated
Heterosexual
Serial Killer
Has Access to
(That You Don't)

"Moral disapproval of a group does not justify discrimination." —U.S. Supreme Court, *Lawrence v. Texas,* 2003

The U.S. Supreme Court long ago determined that the right to marry the person of one's choice was a fundamental civil right, and therefore the government is generally not permitted to set up roadblocks or otherwise second-guess whether marriage is a good idea for any particular couple. There is no limit to the number of marriages one may enter into in one's lifetime. There are no rules requiring people to marry for a specific reason (such as love or procreation), nor are there any rules against people marrying solely to upset one's parents or for money, publicity, or fame. The sole requirement being pushed by religious zealots is to limit marriage to a man and a woman—which is a nice way of putting up a sign that says: NO QUEERS ALLOWED.

Is the Massachusetts Supreme Judicial Court Decision the End of the Rainbow?

On November 18, 2003 the Massachusetts Supreme Judicial Court ruled that "the Massachusetts Constitution affirms the dignity and equality of all individuals. It forbids the creation of second-class citizens." The court found that the government simply lacked any rational basis for denying same-sex couples marriage licenses. But unlike in Canada, where the court ordered clerks to immediately begin providing marriage licenses to same-sex couples, the Massachusetts court issued a 180-day stay on issuing licenses "to permit the legislature to take such action as it may deem appropriate in light of this opinion."

Huh?

The decision left the country perplexed. What did the judges mean and why the 180-day stay? After the Massachusetts governor, attorney general, and state legislature proposed a civil union status, the courts clarified on Feb. 4, 2004, "the dissimilitude between the terms 'civil marriage' and 'civil union' is not innocuous. It is a considered choice of language that reflects a demonstrable assigning of same-sex couples to a second-class status."

On May 17, 2004, the 50th anniversary of the historic *Brown v. Board of Education* ruling that separate is not equal, Massachusetts is poised to become the first state in the United States to grant marriage licenses to same-sex couples. On this date a new American revolution will take place. As this book goes to press, states are scrambling to pass additional laws to deny married same-sex couples legal recognition.

Domestic Partnerships, Civil Unions, Reciprocal Beneficiaries = Fool's Gold

Domestic partnerships, reciprocal beneficiaries, and civil unions may look like progress for same-sex couples, but the reality is that these separate and unequal institutions are Turtle Wax consolation prizes. As the Native Americans learned, be wary of politicians bearing gifts to your people. These newly minted institutions attempt to buy off the gay community at bargain-basement prices.

ALOHA!

What about the Hawaii Supreme Court, which declared in 1993 that Hawaii's state constitution prohibited marriage discrimination? The court failed to immediately require that clerks provide licenses to same-sex couples—and the decision was overruled shortly thereafter by a state ballot initiative changing the constitution. The only rights provided to same-sex couples are "reciprocal beneficiary" benefits that even fall short of the limited protections available in California.

WHAT ABOUT VERMONT? CAN'T GAYS AND LESBIANS GET MARRIED THERE?

The Vermont Supreme Court determined that its state constitution prohibited marriage discrimination in 2000, right? Yes, but the same court explicitly authorized the state legislature to fix the problem. The result? A new term called "civil unions," which provides the state rights afforded married couples, but none of the 1,138 federal rights. By creating a new term, the legislature short-circuited the possibility that relationship equality would join maple syrup as a sweet export out of Vermont. Since there is no such thing as civil unions in any other state, no other state need worry about providing civil union protections.

Vermont civil unions provide same-sex couples with only certain state rights (approximately 300), which is less than 25% of the rights of heterosexual married couples. That is why presidential candidates can say: "I support the individual state's right to choose." That way, they don't have to do anything to get you the other 75% of your rights. Pretty tricky, huh?

CALIFORNIA DREAMIN'?

California—thought to be extremely progressive on the issue of protections for same-sex couples—offers registered domestic partners only 15 of the 300 state rights afforded married couples. Those 15 rights consist of the following:

1. The right to make medical decisions for your partner
2. Hospital visitation
3. Right to file for state disability benefits on behalf of a disabled partner
4. Right to be appointed conservator and to make legal and financial decisions for an incapacitated partner
5. Right to use stepparent adoption procedures
6. Right to inherit if a partner dies without a will
7. Right to sue for wrongful death and infliction of emotional distress if a partner is killed or injured
8. Ability to use form wills and right to automatic appointment as administrator of a partner's estate
9. Right to draft a will or trust for a partner
10. Right to paid leave or to use sick leave to care for a seriously ill partner or a partner's child
11. Right to unemployment insurance if one has to relocate for a partner's job promotion
12. Right to continued health insurance coverage for domestic partners and children of deceased state employees and retirees
13. Right to death benefits for surviving partners of county employees in selected counties
14. Right to live with your partner in senior citizen housing developments

15. No state income tax on employer-provided health
    benefits for domestic partners

These 15 constitute a mere 5% of the total California
state rights available to married couples—and include
none of the 1,138 federal rights. Effective January 1, 2005,
California will add most other state rights enjoyed by married couples but none of the federal rights nor the possibility that these rights will transfer to any other state.

Same-sex couples are effectively marooned on the
islands of Vermont, California, and Hawaii. Leave these
states and you risk jeopardizing the limited protections
provided to your family.

LIP SERVICE

What about those gay-friendly presidential candidates who
stop short of supporting full marriage equality? Instead they
declare support for civil unions or claim the choice of whether
to allow same-sex couples the right to marry should be left up
to individual states. There are major problems with this
ostrich-head-in-the-sand approach. There is no time to carve
out a middle ground on this issue. To say "I believe in equality for LGBT people but believe civil marriage should be limited to a man and a woman" is a contradiction. It's also disingenuous. Either you're on board for full equality or not.

Despite attempts to shift emphasis on marriage away
from the federal government, the fact remains that the federal government is steeped in the marriage business.
Seventy-five percent of the rights that come with civil marriage *are* federal rights.

"SO WHAT ARE ALL THESE RIGHTS ANYWAY?"

While by no means comprehensive, the National
Center for Lesbian Rights (NCLR) has compiled the

brochure "Left at the Altar" in an attempt to shine light on the inequities gays and lesbians face because they lack legal access to marriage. Below are grouped listings of some of the provisions associated with civil marriage.

From NCLR's "Left at the Altar"

Laws Protecting Married Couples in the Event of Death
1. Laws protecting inheritance rights of surviving spouses
2. Laws protecting a surviving spouse's right to bereavement leave
3. Laws protecting the property rights of surviving spouses
4. Laws providing Social Security and workers' compensation benefits for surviving spouses
5. Pension and tax laws protecting surviving spouses
6. Laws protecting burial rights of surviving spouses
7. Laws protecting decision-making authority of surviving spouse over remains and funeral arrangements
8. Laws protecting surviving spouses of firefighters and police officers
9. Laws protecting surviving spouses of veterans

Laws Protecting the Marital Relationship
1. Laws requiring spouses to support and care for each other
2. Laws permitting spouses to take medical leave to care for each other
3. Laws requiring spouses to be responsible for each other's debts
4. Tax laws protecting married couples
5. Laws protecting spouses in the event of disability
6. Laws protecting spouses' testimonial privileges
7. Laws establishing the right to protect one's spouse
8. Laws relating to absentee ballots
9. Laws relating to insurance coverage for spouses

Laws Protecting Spouses in the Event of Divorce
Laws Protecting the Children of Married Couples
1. Laws holding both spouses responsible as legal parents
2. Laws requiring parents to support and care for their children
3. Laws for determining custody and visitation in the event of separation or divorce
4. Laws prohibiting parents from formally dissolving their relationship without meeting the legal requirements of divorce

Laws Related to Incarcerated Persons
Laws Protecting Spouses of Public Officials
Of course, many of us might be thinking, *Well, what the heck do I care about laws relating to incarcerated persons? Those folks get what they deserve.*

Let me put it to you this way:

Q: What do a serial rapist, a murderer, a child pornographer, a lifer, and an armed bank robber share in common?

A: As long as they are heterosexual, they can all get married in prison and never even have to live with their spouses—and you can't!

Incarcerated gays and lesbians with registered domestic partners are not even allowed to have conjugal visits, nor are they allowed to engage in public affection with their partners during regular visits. But their heterosexual convict counterparts can.

PILLOW TALK
The right of marital privilege prevents married individuals from having to testify against their spouses. One can-

not be forced to reveal details of spousal conversations or be required to turn over private correspondence—no matter how key that evidence would be to a lawsuit, either criminal or civil. Think that would never come up in your life? I wonder if Rosie O'Donnell ever gave this a second thought before her legal battle with magazine publisher Gruner & Jahr USA.

Since Rosie and her partner, Kelli, cannot legally marry, Kelli was compelled to testify as to the content of their conversations and even to turn over their personal e-mails! In response to the publisher's attorney's questions, Kelli prefaced her replies with an indirect protest: "In the privacy of our home, between the two us, just as any spouse would go home and talk to their other half about a bad day at work—yeah, we had that conversation."

Rosie had this to say: "Kelli and I are not legally married, nor are we allowed any kind of title that gives us the validation of who in fact we are: a family. Any and all correspondence that Kelli and I had was allowed to be entered into evidence—while any and all correspondence our married CEO had with his wife was not required to be disclosed."

WHAT BROWN WON'T DO FOR YOU

Daniel and Frank had been together for 27 years when Frank's employer, United Airlines, closed its San Francisco office and relocated its employees to Chicago. Daniel, who had worked for United Parcel Service for 20 years, requested a transfer to UPS's Chicago office. But, according to Lambda Legal, "although UPS has a policy that allows employees to transfer to other offices to follow a spouse, UPS refused to allow Daniel to transfer because he and Frank are not legally married." Despite the fact that the two live in a state with domestic partnership benefits, because they have no access to a civil marriage license, Daniel and Frank have had to live apart from each other, at great emotional and financial cost.

AND THE LIST GOES ON...

Each of the thousands of marriage rights is meaningful. Couples who are denied access to them can suffer devastating consequences. While we may not ever personally experience these types of injustices, someone we care about might. My friends Julie and Maggie never worried about being denied the right to a "loss of consortium" claim (don't worry, I'll explain) until a cab sped through a red light and struck Julie while she was commuting to work on her motorcycle. Julie managed to survive the accident with broken ribs, two broken legs, and a broken arm. Maggie was pregnant at the time and experiencing outrageous morning sickness; she was dependent on Julie for physical, emotional, and financial support. Suddenly, Julie was unable to provide for the couple. When Julie was finally able to return home after eight weeks in the hospital, Maggie had to take care of her.

Graced with the love and support of their local Episcopal Church, Maggie and Julie made it through the most difficult time in their lives. Members of the parish provided a never-ending supply of hot dishes and supportive visits. When Julie was finally well again and the pregnancy was going smoother, Maggie contacted an attorney. She was ready to deal with the civil aspect of the suit against the careless cabby who'd almost killed her wife. To her dismay, she learned that one of the rights denied same-sex couples was loss of consortium.

"Loss of consortium" means that damages are paid to the spouse of an injured party whose injuries render him or her unable to provide emotional, physical, financial, or even sexual support. This is something heterosexual couples can take for granted. Ironically, Maggie was told that because of the Sharon Smith case, had Julie died, she would be able to sue for wrongful death, but that, to date, there was no such ruling on loss of consortium. In other words: tough luck.

It may sound petty, but the psychic damages and hardship Julie and Maggie faced were no less serious than if they had been a heterosexual couple in the same situation. If Julie had been a man, Maggie would have received compensation for her suffering. I can just hear the plaintiff's attorney for the heterosexual married couple espousing the added tragedy that the husband was unable to care for his pregnant wife and his injuries added additional stress to her pregnancy, increasing the risk to her and the baby. Where are our advocates?

> *"Homosexual activists say they need legal status so they can visit their partners in hospitals, etc. But hospitals leave visitation up to the patient except in very rare instances. This 'issue' is a smoke screen to cover the fact that, using legal instruments such as power of attorney, drafting a will, etc., homosexuals can share property, designate heirs, dictate hospital visitors, and give authority for medical decisions. What they should not obtain is identical recognition and support for a relationship that is not equally essential to society's survival."*
> —Robert Knight, a draftsman of the 1996 Federal Defense of Marriage Act

A lot of people think that gays and lesbians can just get good legal documentation to cover these 1,138 rights. I hate to be the bearer of bad news again, but this is completely false. Just contact the National Center for Lesbian Rights, Lambda Legal, or a top gay and lesbian family rights attorney, and they'll all tell you the same thing: You'll need more than a good lawyer.

Federal rights and protections that come with marriage can only be given by a higher authority. The only state rights for same-sex couples have come through legislation (California domestic partnerships) or litigation (Vermont civil unions).

Good Sharon

In January 2001, Sharon Smith, a vice president for Charles Schwab, was living with her partner of seven years, Diane Whipple. Diane was attacked and killed by her neighbors' dogs, which were known throughout the apartment building to be vicious and aggressive. Sharon wanted to sue the dogs' owners, Marjorie Knoller and Robert Noel, for Diane's wrongful death, believing the two had acted irresponsibly. But, for Sharon, proving her case was not as challenging as learning that she had no right to bring this kind of lawsuit, because she and Diane were not legally married.

Sharon was shocked and outraged. The brutality of Diane's preventable death, coupled with the lack of remorse by the dogs' owners and the knowledge that she was considered a legal stranger to her spouse was too much to take sitting down. She dove headfirst into bringing the country out of what had been previously only a faint dialogue on same-sex couples' rights.

An accidental activist, Sharon became committed to seeking justice for her beloved. Diane's death was a tragic loss to all who loved her, but it also increased public awareness of the insults same-sex couples face by not being able to marry. This awareness also touched the judge hearing Sharon's plea. He changed the course of history by agreeing that Sharon should be able to sue for wrongful death just like any other spouse.

Sharon's story also moved the California legislature to enact, and Governor Davis to sign, AB 25, which gave registered domestic partners in California the right to sue for wrongful death and 13 other important rights. (A 14th, inheritance, was added the next year.)

While the victory was sweet, it was equally made bitter by the fact that a young woman had to die so violently just to get lawmakers and justices to sit up and take notice. Worse yet, until our nation grants us the right to marry, numerous men and women outside of California and Vermont (and possibly Massachusetts) will face similar hardships.

BAD SHARON

Around the same time and also in California, there was another lesbian named Sharon who decided to use the homophobia of the law against her ex-partner. In the Sharon S. case, Sharon argued that her ex-partner did not have parental rights to their younger son because a) the child was not hers biologically; and b) the child had not yet been officially adopted by her ex when they split. Yet the two women had planned having the child together and they were already co-parenting another child. Sharon's partner had also been intimately involved in the care of the child until their separation. Nevertheless, the California Court of Appeal ruled in Bad Sharon's favor. If the couple had been married heterosexuals, the point would have been moot. The nonbiological parent would have been considered a legal parent under the California Family Code. (Almost a year later the

California Supreme Court reversed the ruling.)

Currently in California, a nonbiological parent in a registered domestic partnership must adopt his or her child after the child's birth. The process is expensive, lengthy, and involves a home visit. On the other hand, a nonbiological parent in a civil marriage is automatically the child's parent at birth—no fee, no home visit, no second-class status.

WHAT DO A NAVAJO POLICE OFFICER, AN ASIAN ENGINEER, A CAUCASIAN FLORIST, A BLACK ATTORNEY, AND A LATINA LIBRARIAN ALL HAVE IN COMMON?

That's right: If they're all gay, they can't legally marry their sweethearts.

Marriage discrimination cuts across all race, ethnic, and class backgrounds. We will all know the pain of being turned away at the marriage license counter when we step up with our beloved and ask for a form. We will all be told that we will need to return with an opposite-sex partner.

One year my wife, Molly McKay, and I asked for a marriage license at the San Francisco City Hall. We were standing in line in front of two gay men, a binational couple. We approached the counter and asked for a marriage license. When the clerk denied us, we turned around and each linked arms with the man behind us and re-approached the counter. This time the clerk immediately handed us a form. "We don't even know these men," I said. "We've been together for six years and you won't let us marry, but we can each marry a complete stranger off the street?"

"One man, one woman," the clerk replied coldly.

The people behind us waiting for their "real marriages" had enough of our silly shenanigans and grew impatient. We were imposing on their romantic day!

four

The Language
of Love

"No one writes love songs about domestic partner-ships!" —Molly McKay, J.D., wife of the author and executive director of Marriage Equality California

---

How Romantic!

"Marge and I are going to be domestic partners!"
"Will you civil-union me?"
"I love my reciprocal beneficiary!"
"Do you take Rudy to be your lawfully registered domestic partner?"
"My reciprocal beneficiary and I are going to the Bahamas after our commitment ceremony."

Let's face it: No matter how hard you try, you can't make the term *domestic partner* sound sexy, romantic, or spiritual. The designation—which sounds more like a housecleaning service than a term of endearment—doesn't even come close to what is expressed by the nouns *husband* and *wife*, or even the gender-neutral *spouse*. You aren't going to find a Hallmark card with a message that begins "To my domestic partner," nor will we ever sing songs about "going to the city hall and getting civil-unioned." For God's sake, *unioned* isn't even a verb. It's not even a word!

There's a vast emotional expanse between talking about your *wife* or *husband*—two roles that are clear in almost every culture—versus talking about your *partner*. I've had more than one person think I'd just started a small business when I introduced Molly that way. And, for the same reason, I'm sure some hapless people still think I'm a lawyer at her firm.

There's no such confusion with the terms *husband* and *wife*. They are clear, emotion-laden, significance-bearing terms—honorific titles even—that have until recently been reserved only for heterosexuals. That's why many straight people turn their heads when I introduce Molly as my wife. They look at me like I just farted. (I have to say, though, I've seen this look on many a lesbian feminist's face too!)

The language of love has power, and we have been given a very slim piece of the pie and asked to stay in our corner of the room and eat it quietly. The message is half "Please don't remind us that we gave you anything," and half "Don't you dare start asking for an equal share."

"Society uses marriage as shorthand to decide who gets to share and who does not."
E.J. Graff, author of *What Is Marriage For?*

We all grew up in a time when gay sex was illegal someplace, when many Americans thought of us as mentally ill freaks who molested children. And while it may not be proper to say it out loud, my hunch is that quite a few straight Americans still believe we are.

Decades upon decades of misinformation, invisibility, and persecution have negatively affected our self-esteem, severely damaged our psyche, and led us to believe we should be grateful for any bone society is willing to toss. How can we possibly push the *m* word on those who have come to tolerate us? I know a guy—and you probably do too—who feels lucky that he can simply walk down the street without worrying about getting his head bashed in, so long as he isn't too flamboyant.

Believe me, I've been there too. But enough already! Until we start demanding to be treated like every other taxpayer who has access to marriage, the Scouts, the military, and other social institutions, whether we're personally interested in them or not, we will not be treated equally.

Full access + full marriage rights = full citizenship

We live a half-existence compared to our heterosexual friends. When they start dating, people watch and wait. Will they graduate from *boyfriend* and *girlfriend* to *fiancé* and *fiancée*? When the two become *husband* and *wife*, their importance to each other graduates to a level even strangers can understand. Each is now also elevated in the eyes of society and family, and thus welcomed into a network of relatedness: *husband, son-in-law, brother-in-law, uncle*, etc... Each is now connected to a larger clan. Marriage is an age-old ritual—and one of the most pivotal of adulthood.

Gay and lesbian Americans, on the other hand, are left out of this widespread global fraternity. We come out, but if any of us get into a relationship, there is often no acknowledgment of its value. We are asked about our *friend* or our *roommate*. OK, so maybe in some places people have progressed and are more comfortable using *girlfriend* or *boyfriend*. But, hey, a *girlfriend* is what you have in high school, or someone you have an affair with, or hook up with after a divorce.

A *girlfriend* is *not* someone you have been with for 30 years.

Come on, when do we get to grow up? We are denied access to a rite of passage that helps us let go of our own selfishness and take on the responsibility of caring for our beloved. We are denied the state protections and family support to care for each other and to make our relationships vibrant, healthy, and long-lasting.

And what about the challenges families face in not knowing how to integrate those "special friends," "significant others," "girlfriends," and "boyfriends" into their lives—challenges that could so easily be solved by giving all citizens equal access to civil marriage.

"OK, I Get It! But Still...Why "Marriage"? Can't We Call It Something Else?"

Legal terms such as *domestic partners*, *reciprocal beneficiaries*, and *civil unions* originated partly because many people thought they would be less offensive to the straight community. However, not only do these concepts come with fewer rights, they don't travel. And the religious right wants to ban *them* too!

"You never hear any parent saying I want to dance at my daughter's commitment ceremony!"
**—Evan Wolfson, J.D., executive director,
Freedom to Marry Collaborative, New York**

Commitment ceremonies may initially be less threatening to us, and to non-gay peers and families, but everyone understands the concept and tradition of a wedding and its meaning. On the other hand, there is no cultural prescription for a commitment ceremony. "You may now kiss your reciprocal beneficiary" sounds nice—well, at least interesting—but "You may now kiss your bride" sounds a lot better. Consider "I now pronounce you domestic partners!" versus "I now pronounce you husband and husband!"

What rhymes with domestic partner?

Is it fair that Alison is expected to call her brother's "wife" of one day her *sister-in-law*, when her "partner" of seven years is just *my sister's friend* to him? Ouch! Is it fair that in Wyoming (or any other state outside of California), authors Del Martin and Phyllis Lyon, who have been together for 50 years, are legal strangers?

Remember this: Marriage is not just a word. It's a word embedded in a whole cultural system that we are daily asked to participate in, while being excluded from. Marriage equality is about people, regardless of sexual orientation, having access to the same rights, responsibilities, protections, and obligations as every other married couple. When LGBT people become able to legally marry, they will be married, not *gay-married*, and not *same-sex-married*. They'll just be simply *married*.

five

Why Marriage Lite Doesn't Work

"We are not seeking special treatment. We seek equality. We are asking that the marriage laws be applied equally to all couples, regardless of sexual orientation. That is the only gay agenda—equality for everyone under the law." —Rev. Troy Perry, Metropolitan Community Church, Los Angeles

As mentioned previously, there are approximately 1,400 rights (300+ on average per state and 1,138 federal) that come with civil marriage. Civil unions (Vermont) provide for all the available state rights, while domestic partnerships (California) and reciprocal beneficiaries (Hawaii) provide for only a few selected rights at this time. Local counties of these states may provide their government workers with the right to share healthcare benefits, but the buck stops there.

Even if Massachusetts allows same-sex couples to marry, those marriages need not be recognized in other states, nor will those couples receive federal protections such as Social Security, Medicare, family leave, health care, disability, or military benefits.

Alternatives to marriage are inherently unequal. Approximately 75% of the rights conferred through civil marriage come from federal marriage laws. No state can possibly come close to giving same-sex couples equitable rights until the federal Defense of Marriage Act (DOMA) is repealed. The DOMA—signed into law by Pres. Bill Clinton in 1996 and defining marriage as "a legal union between one man and one woman"—can block any advances of federal marriage rights for same-sex couples, regardless of what euphemisms we use. Therefore, it's meaningless for the 2004 presidential nominees to say they "support the state's right to choose," because they know it doesn't matter what the state does. What matters is what happens federally with the Defense of Marriage Act.

> # Marriage:
> ## It's accepted in 50 states and around the world.
> # Marriage:
> ## It's everywhere you want to be.

While the term *domestic partner* is applied in various cities and counties throughout the country, unless you have registered with the California Domestic Partnership registry, are a resident of California, and are currently within the state boundaries of California, your domestic partnership rights are null and void. That's right! Once you leave the California border, you have no legal rights. Yes, even on a day trip, you are subject to the laws of whatever state you're in.

Why? Well, 38 states have mini-DOMAs so that they cannot be required to recognize any relationship that is not between a man and a woman. They don't have to let you into the hospital room of your domestic partner who's been stricken with a heart attack. They don't have to allow you the right to sue for wrongful death. They don't have to tell you that your partner is being held in a psychiatric hospital. They don't have to let you authorize or not authorize medical treatment of your partner's children. They don't have to allow you to control disposition of your lover's remains.

Basically, they don't have to consider you as anything other than a legal stranger.

Scenario 1

You are a resident of California and a registered domestic partner. If you are walking down any street in California and get hit by a reckless driver and killed, your partner will be able to sue for your wrongful death.

Scenario 2

You are a resident of California and a registered domestic partner. If you are walking down any street anywhere else in the USA and get hit by a reckless bus driver and killed, your partner will *not* be able to sue for your wrongful death in that state.

Again, domestic partnership rights and civil union rights **DO NOT LEAVE THE STATE**. According to a 2003 report from the Human Rights Campaign (HRC), some folks in New Hampshire decided to be somewhat friendly to traveling Vermonters and proposed a House Bill that would recognize civil unions only for "health-care decisions during stays in the state of not more than 30 days."

Well, isn't that generous! If at the end of your two week trip to New Hampshire your partner has a stroke and ends up in the hospital, you then have two weeks to get him or her back to Vermont or your next of kin rights will turn into a pumpkin!

I recall a heterosexual friend of mine who was visiting family on the East Coast when her husband had a stroke and required two months hospitalization before they could stabilize him enough to get him on a plane back to California. It would be outrageous for medical staff or the government to tell her that after 30 days she would lose her right to make medical decisions for him and that that right would be handed over to someone else.

> *"We tried 'separate but equal' in this country once before. It didn't work. The water fountains may have been dispensing water from the same source, but the social segregation reinforced the second-class status of an entire group of citizens. Aside from all the practical and legal reasons that you can't create two separate family institutions and call them equal. It is simply NOT equality to segregate families into different systems when we already have a civil institution that could apply to everyone. AB 205 was pragmatic. Equality requires marriage."*
> —Toni Broaddus, Program Director, Equality California

SEPARATE IS INHERENTLY UNEQUAL

In 1954, *Brown v. Board of Education* established that "separate was not equal." You cannot create two separate institutions and have parity. Yet, despite the U.S. Supreme Court's message with regard to racial discrimination, many people want to revisit injustice by creating alternatives to marriage. Surprisingly, the frothing right wingers don't wish to do this (they're against any and all rights for

LGBT people), the moderates do; and they are joined even by radical left-wingers who, believing marriage to be a doomed institution, want to protect LGBT people from the dangers of cultural assimilation.

"Why should straights be the only ones to have their unenforceable promise to love, honor, and cherish trap them like houseflies in the web of law? Marriage will not only open up to gay men and lesbians whole new vistas of guilt, frustration, claustrophobia, bewilderment, declining self-esteem, unfairness, and sorrow, it will offer them the opportunity to prolong this misery by tormenting each other in court."
—Katha Pollitt

So many people, regardless of where their sexual orientation falls on the Kinsey Scale, say that marriage is a failed institution. Why does that have to be true for LGBT people? Heck, we've been sitting on the sidelines all this time. We haven't even had our turn.

Marriage is simply a choice to which all of us should have access. In the same way that a choice to remain single or to cohabit should be equally respectable.

SEPARATE BUT UNEQUAL AT WORK IN CALIFORNIA

While domestic partnerships in California are a huge breakthrough when compared with the legal rights offered same-sex couples in other states, the implementation of the registration is confusing. The current process actually makes it harder for same-sex couples to register as domestic partners than for heterosexuals to obtain marriage licenses.

For example, domestic partner applicants commonly go to their local county recorder's office to obtain a form. It seems to make sense, right? Why wouldn't they just hand the gay people domestic partnership forms and the hetero couples marriage licenses? Well, because that would be too easy! Often—though not consistently—domestic partnership applicants must go to City Hall. So, after waiting in long lines, many are told they are in the wrong place.

Once the applicants finally get to City Hall, several things can happen:

1. The clerk can erroneously register the couple only for that city, misleading the couple to believe that they are registered with the state. Usually, this goes undiscovered until one of the important rights that comes with the state register is needed such as the right to inherit without a will, right to stepparent adoption, etc, often with catastrophic results.

2. The City Hall clerk does not have the statewide domestic partnership forms or even the most basic information about where to get them, not even the Web address where the form can be downloaded. This leaves couples utterly confused as to how to register as domestic partners, reducing the likelihood that they ever will.

3. If the couple is in luck and their City Hall has a copy of the form, they must still go to the trouble of having it notarized. Then they must mail the form to the Secretary of State. Perhaps the couple will misplace the form, or it will get lost in the mail, or they will send it without the notary signature, or they will be too embarrassed to take the form to a notary, or they will not be able to find or

pay for the notary on the same day that they pick up the form. All these stumbling blocks can postpone the registry even longer—and don't think potential domestic partners don't get cold feet!

All these what-ifs are not true for married couples who are able to complete the license process at the counter and are not required to have their license notarized. Nor do they need to mail in the form. That is done for them—compliments of the state.

A Civil Union Is Not a Marriage

Similarly, a Vermont civil union is not a marriage. Same-sex couples in Vermont pay the same amount for their civil union license that heterosexual couples do for a marriage license. However, same-sex couples are given a certificate indicating a civil union, not a civil marriage, a new term that has none of the emotional connotation or prestige of marriage.

As with California domestic partnerships, the same-sex couple's civil union loses its validity at the border, nontransferable to neighboring New Hampshire, Massachusetts, and New York, with the possible exception of couples who relocate to Manhattan; they may not have to pay an additional fee to become registered domestic partners in New York City. Heterosexuals married in Vermont, however, have relationships that are recognized not only in the three neighboring states but in all 50 states and U.S. territories. Why should the government grant some privileges, but not all? Why should same-sex couples pay the same fees—and sometimes even more—for less than 25% of the rights heterosexuals have?

"Marriage lite" alternatives are inherently separate and

unequal. Only full marriage equality will grant same-sex couples all of the nearly 1,400 state and federal rights of civil marriage, eliminating loopholes and inequities in one fell swoop.

six

Taxes
and Death

"We pay our bills, we pay our taxes, yet you deny us marriage access!" —Marriage Equality California chant, April 15, 2002, Tax Day Protest

Gay couples—whether or not they are registered domestic partners—pay inheritance taxes on their partners' estates. Heterosexual married couples are exempt. We also pay death taxes in the 24 states that have death taxes because we are legal strangers to our life partners. No gay or lesbian in a committed relationship can file as "head of household" on his or her federal or state income tax form. We can't claim exemptions for our nonbiological children, unless we've gone through a lengthy second-parent adoption. And we get taxed extra on our domestic partners' health insurance benefits.

30 Years Together and Still Filing Single!

"Some people wait until they get married to have sex. We've been having sex and are still waiting to get married." —Shelly Bailes and Ellen Pontac, together since November 19, 1973

The Internal Revenue Service expects adults who have been in a committed relationship for 30 years, like Shelly and Ellen, to check "single" when they do their taxes. Federal tax law denies them the right to file jointly. At present, the IRS doesn't even extend the courtesy of putting faux categories like "domestic partner" or "joined in a civil union" on the form. Folks who are legally married in other countries, such as Canada, are expected to come back to the U.S. and check "single"—or risk incarceration and tax evasion if they don't.

INHERITANCE TAX

When a person dies, the federal government places a tax on all property and assets owned by the deceased that can be as high as 50% of the total value of the assets. A number of states then have a separate state death tax on top of the federal government tax that must also be paid before the beneficiaries of the will get anything.

However, federal tax law authorizes a marital deduction that exempts all property left outright to a surviving spouse.

"So," some might say, "the only real asset we have is our house—which we own as joint tenants. So we don't have to pay any estate tax on that do we?" Oh, yes, you do. The total value of all property held in joint tenancy is included in a taxable estate, minus the portion the surviving joint tenant can prove s/he contributed. Unmarried couples are also, in most places, hit with property tax reassessment upon the death of one partner.

Every surviving same-sex joint tenant risks losing his or her home to estate taxes.

So, if you own a half-interest in the home you and your partner purchased for $150,000, and the value went up to $350,000 over a period of 15 years, you would be taxed on your partner's half-interest in a $350,000 home. Many unmarried couples have lost a beloved piece of property, their most important investment, as a result of this scenario.

This is not so for surviving widows or widowers. Rather, the taxes are deferred until the death of the surviving partner as well.

TILL DEATH DO US PART WITH OUR RIGHTS

As if taxation without equal representation wasn't enough! With death comes a whole new list of uncertainties and lack of protections.

BURIAL AND FUNERAL ARRANGEMENTS

Who is authorized to make funeral and burial arrangements? The family, the so-called next of kin. But are you, as the surviving partner of a same-sex relationship, recognized as family? Only if you are in a Vermont civil union, a Hawaiian reciprocal beneficiary, or a California domestic partnership (after January 1, 2005). Otherwise, you'll most likely be considered a legal stranger with no more rights over your partner's body than the neighbor you've never met.

What are the practical implications of being a legal stranger? You cannot view the body. You cannot direct whether your partner will be buried, cremated, or donated to science. You cannot arrange the funeral—in fact, if the family wants to get nasty, they may fly his or her body to their home state, and not even tell you when it's scheduled.

We have seen many cases where surviving partners think they have the right to make decisions...but they don't. We have seen the family of the partner who has passed elbow the surviving partner away. It's heartbreaking for us!
—Alison Rodman, Chapel of the Chimes, Oakland, Calif.

How can you rest in peace when your partner may be fighting with your family about funeral arrangements and burial decisions? You've heard the horror stories: "There was this really beautiful drag queen who never wore a suit in his life, but his parents insisted he be buried in one" or "I know this butch lesbian who wouldn't be caught dead in a dress, but she'll be wearing Laura Ashley for all eternity."

These horror stories are everyday truths. In almost every state, burial rights and funeral arrangements go to the spouse first, then to the next of kin, a term that does not include same-sex partners. That's right. Even if you've been in the relationship for 50 years, if he or she dies and does not have a will and an advanced health care directive, your partner's family members (i.e. niece, nephew, sibling, or even a third cousin) will be the ones to decide where your loved one will spend eternity and what he or she will be wearing when they do.

It may seem like kind of a strange thing to think about now, but when you find yourself in this type of unthinkable dilemma—reeling from grief, helpless to abide by your partner's wishes—you awaken to the true viciousness of the law.

THE SOCIAL SECURITY RIP-OFF

"Most of us don't like to talk about death or even think about it. But wouldn't you feel better knowing that, if you were no longer living, Social Security would help take care of your family? Of course, you would."
    —Social Security Web page advertisement

Of course we'd feel more comfortable knowing that our survivors would have access to the fund we've been contributing to *all* our working lives and that they would be able to live as comfortably as possible in the same homes and within the same means as they had during our lifetimes. But for LGBT people, Social Security as a part of the retirement equation is not an option. One of the most mean-spirited aspects of the "Denial of Marriage Act" signed by President Clinton is that same-sex survivors will continue to be denied the Social Security benefits of their mates, forcing lavender seniors to live without the resources available to their heterosexual counterparts—regardless of progressive state laws.

"The loss of the family wage earner can be devastating to the survivors."
    —SSA Publication No. 05-10084, August 2001

"Some of the Social Security taxes you pay go towards survivors insurance. In fact, the value of the survivors insurance you have under Social Security is probably more than the value of your individual life insurance."
    —SSA Publication No. 05-10084, August 2001

"There is a special one-time payment of $225 that can be made when you die if you have enough work credits. This payment can be made only to your spouse or minor children if they meet certain requirements."
—SSA Publication No. 05-10084, August 2001

Do gay Americans have less of a work ethic? Do we put less time into our chosen fields of employment than our straight colleagues? Did we work any less hard to earn those pensions? Did we not fork over an equal share of our salaries?

Let's crunch numbers just to show you how big a bite this denial of Social Security benefits takes out of our monthly incomes at a time when we are already in financial jeopardy. Log on to www.ssa.gov and click on the link to "calculate your benefits." Type in your age and salary and you will learn just how much money your partner is cheated out of because you can't make him or her your legal spouse.

Example 1*

If you were born January 1, 1960, and made **$25,000** a year and had died in November 2003, your unrecognized spouse would be denied **$892 a month** at normal retirement age, which is usually 67. If your spouse was caring for your child, he or she would be denied **$678 a month** in child survivor's benefits.

Example 2

If you were born January 1, 1960, and made **$50,000 a year** and had died in November 2003, your unrecognized spouse would be denied **$1,430 a month** at normal retirement age. If the U.S. government honored your relationship, then your spouse caring for your child would receive **$1,072 a month** in child survivor's benefits.

Example 3

If you were born January 1, 1960 and made **$75,000 a year** and had died in November 2003, your unrecognized spouse would be denied **$1,738 a month** at normal retirement age. If you were legally married, your spouse caring for your child would receive **$1,303 a month** in child survivor's benefits.

Example 4

If you were born January 1, 1960 and made **$100,000 a year** and had died in November 2003, your unrecognized spouse would be denied **$1,948 a month** at normal retirement age. Your spouse caring for your child would be denied **$1,461 a month** in child survivor's benefits.

(*Examples taken from www.ssa.gov/cgi-bin/benefit4.cgi on November 4, 2003.)

Social Security benefits are even available to *divorced* heterosexuals!

"Social Security pays survivor benefits to widows and widowers but not to the surviving same-sex partner of someone who dies. This may cost GLBT elders $124 million a year in un-accessed benefits. Medicaid regulations protect the assets and homes of married spouses when the other spouse enters a nursing home or long-term care facility; no such protections are offered to same-sex partners. Tax laws and other regulations of 401K's and pensions discriminate against same-sex partners, costing the

*surviving partner tens of thousands of dollars a year,
and possibly over $1 million during the course of a
lifetime. This is particularly striking when one
takes into consideration that, even with full access
to benefits, 11% of all elders live below the poverty level and another 6% are classified as near-poor.
And same-sex partners are often denied even the
most basic rights such as hospital visitation or the
right to live or die in the same nursing home."*
—National Gay and Lesbian Task Force,
Key Policy Recommendations for GLBT Elders

But hey, it's just money. And besides marriage is between
a man and a woman, for hets only. Why would queer people want to participate in something so patriarchal? After
all, it's more important to be cool and socially noncon-
formist than it is to make sure that our lavender seniors can
pay their rents and aren't homeless. There's no need for
those of us under 50 to have to even think about all those
geeky things like retirement and Social Security anyway.

FIREFIGHTERS, POLICE OFFICERS, CORRECTIONAL WORKERS—OH, MY!

Every day uniformed public employees put their lives
on the line to protect us from criminals, terrorists, and
natural disasters. In return for their heroic acts these
individuals are granted certain benefits, so that—should
they be injured or killed in the line of duty—their loved
ones will continue to be sustained.

That is, unless they're gay.

*"There was a time in my life when I though human
rights work did not impact me. But in 2001, I lost
my partner of 10 years, Lois Marrero, a fellow police*

officer shot and killed in the line of duty. Despite being married in a church and affirming our lifelong commitment, I was denied the pension benefits due a surviving spouse because our relationship isn't recognized by Florida law. Having my life with Lois denied in such a public way has been painful and demeaning." —Mickie Mashburn

Depending on their state or city, survivors of public servants who are not legally married can be denied death benefits such as monthly annuities to help pay the mortgage or their children's medical bills. They may find themselves having to sell their homes, an option to which heterosexual widows and widowers don't often have to resort. Many gay survivors of firefighters and law enforcement agents are also not able to access scholarship benefits and are routinely denied community recognition.

Lois Marrero and Mickie Mashburn had been together for 10 years and were both police officers in Tampa, Florida. Lois was killed while responding to a robbery. Lois had worked as a police officer for 19 years and was nearing retirement. Though the police chief recognized Mickie as the widow of the slain officer at the funeral and presented her with the flag from Lois's coffin, Mickie was denied the right to Lois's pension. Because they were not allowed to legally marry, Mickie received neither pension *nor Social Security payments* following the death of her partner.

Why should gays have to choose between being good citizens who serve the public and good spouses who provide and protect their families? Don't the two go hand in hand? Those who make these kinds of personal sacrifices— and the partners who support them—should be honored and recognized for it.

PROBLEMS FACED BY 9/11 SURVIVORS

The World Trade Center catastrophe provided a microcosm for the legal inequities between similarly situated surviving partners of married and unmarried couples. Newlywed spouses received hundreds of thousands of dollars in state and federal aid without question. Long-term committed same-sex couples were denied any death benefits. And, really, for the first time, the nation turned its attention to this unfairness and in several surprising cases, remedied the problem...but only for this national tragedy. The general discriminatory rules still apply to all future disasters.

Larry Courtney lost his partner of 14 years, Gene Clark, when a plane hit the South Tower of the World Trade Center. Larry immediately had to move out of the apartment he could no longer afford alone. Because Larry and Gene were not legal spouses, Larry was not eligible to receive up to $20,000 in spousal death benefits under workers' compensation to which a widower would normally be entitled under New York law. Nor was he entitled to Social Security spousal survivor benefits.

Because Gene died without a will, Gene's estranged father stood to inherit all of Gene's assets. Moreover, due to Gene's father's lack of cooperation, Larry was unable to be appointed administrator of Gene's estate. Larry, with the help of Lambda Legal, was able to help apply political pressure such that the New York legislature granted workers' compensation to domestic partners—but only for 9/11 survivors.

Peggy Neff lost her partner of 17 years, Sheila Hines, in the Pentagon attack of 9/11. Sheila was also the primary breadwinner and thought the couple had taken every legal precaution they could to protect each other. Peggy was threatened with the loss of their house if she did not receive proceeds from the Victims Compensation Fund. She applied for disaster relief and received a letter from the Pentagon that expressed condolences for the loss of her "friend" but indicated she did not meet the definition of family established for receiving compensation. After several hearings on the issue, the federal government relented and provided Peggy compensation for Sheila's death, marking the first time the federal government has ever recognized a same-sex partner with the kind of support and protection it provides to married couples.

Only time will tell if these small victories mark a growing trend toward recognition of same-sex couples or are simply one-time acts of altruism sparked by a national tragedy and the prominent roles played in it by gay heroes such as Mark Bingham and Father Mychal Judge.

seven

Monogamy
and Partnership

"There is no more lovely, friendly, and charming relationship, communion or company than a good marriage." —Martin Luther

THE *M* WORD

I'm not sure which *m* word is more threatening: marriage or monogamy. For some in the LGBT community, the two go hand in hand. For others, marriage simply represents an opportunity to have a committed relationship for life—with nonmonogamy being negotiable.

The notion of married nonmonogamy is by no means exclusive to the gay community. Many individuals in heterosexual marriages, though they may have agreed to be monogamous, partake in undisclosed affairs or at least make the occasional field trip to a strip-club or singles bar. And there are quite a few straight-only swingers' clubs; gay people did not invent the term *wife-swapping*.

I believe the monogamous commitment my wife and I have made has provided a strong foundation of trust for our relationship. Of course, we have discussed that bedtime hypothetical question: "What if Angelina Jolie knocked on the front door and begged for one night alone with you?" But seriously, knowing each of us has committed to honoring the other as "enough" provides a level of security that has helped us through our fair share of rough spots.

Being honest with each other and deciding on the rules up front, regarding either monogamy or nonmonogamy, is just as important as what those rules ultimately are, if not more so. Secretive behavior—promising one thing but doing another—undermines the unity and integrity of the relationship. It's common sense.

I am not saying that marriage is right for everyone. However, unlike our straight counterparts who are often pressured, cajoled, bribed, and celebrated for marrying and settling down, gay people often come to the simultaneous and erroneous conclusion that they will never marry and settle down. Just try to picture it: gay married life. What would it look like?

THE BENEFITS OF LIFETIME COMMITMENT

An unpublished study by the San Francisco Department of Health compared two groups of gay men who were in nonmonogamous long-term relationships. The first group consisted of men in registered domestic partnerships; those in the second were not. The study found that men in domestic partnerships were more likely to have safe sex and thus had a reduced risk of getting or giving sexually transmitted diseases than those who had not taken this legal step. If these findings bear out in more extensive studies (and I believe they will), this is a big deal. When gay men's relationships are respected by legal status, they are more likely to respect themselves, their domestic partners, and their other sexual partners.

While there are numerous stresses associated with

being married (picking up your spouse's socks, or having to pay for his Macy's shopping spree, his parking tickets, and his high-risk automobile insurance premiums when you're a Triple A "preferred good driver"), there are also demonstrated positive psychological consequences. Companionship provides a buffer against stress, and a stability that helps people get through the best and worst of life.

BEING GAY IS LIKE PLAYING A PERPETUAL GAME OF MS. PAC-MAN

"When you're gay or lesbian, you can be together for 20 or 30 years and it's almost like you're trapped in this perpetual state of adolescence because you're always dating your partner." —L.J. Carusone, Southern California Executive Director of Marriage Equality California

Have you ever played a broken video game and been unable to get to the next level? The game keeps sending you back to the same one you just aced. Well, being gay in the USA is kind of like playing a broken Ms. Pac-Man. You've eaten all of the dots and cleared the screen, but you just keep going back to the level with the cherries. Now, certainly Level 1 has its perks: boundless bowls of cherries, the thrill of the initial courtship, easy and carefree trails to traverse. But eventually, after you've done your share of spins through the maze (explained to the umpteenth girl the same dream about how you'd like to open a retreat center in Sonoma eventually) you begin to yearn for a new puzzle. How would it be to go deeper?

You realize something: Being stuck at the cherries sucks. The cherries are worth only 100 points, whereas the oranges, bananas, and other higher-level fruits yield substantially better payoffs. The point is that, as gay Americans, no matter how well we do in our relationships, how close we are, or how long we've been together, our society sees us as stuck at Level 1. When the straight folks are playing Ms. Pac-Man, they get to go on to the WEDDING BELLS screen. You know, where Ms. Pac-Man dons a veil and Mr. Pac-Man a bow tie, and they waltz off together into the Technicolor honeymoon? We are stuck at THEY MEET. We just keep bumping our heads and seeing hearts.

eight

Injustice
for All

"Marriage strengthens individuals and society. When you have two people who are willing to be legally responsible for each other, to have each other's best interests at heart, this benefits the entire country." —Jon W. Davidson, Senior Counsel, Lambda Legal Defense and Education Fund

If heterosexuals who are against marriage equality would take a look at the civil laws that come with marriage, they could become some of its biggest proponents. While same-sex couples are denied shared Social Security benefits, immigration sponsorship rights, joint taxation, and a host of other benefits, heterosexual married couples are also being unfairly burdened by the U.S. government.

Welfare, housing, and other benefits require that married heterosexuals report both partners' incomes for determining aid eligibility. Gay partners aren't seen as spouses, so are therefore not included in determining a benefit! Not only do we not have to report our partners' income when seeking government aid, we also don't need to report gifts given to us by lobbying groups just because we are the partner of a government official. It's scandalous isn't it? By providing gay couples with civil marriage rights the government would save money in other areas and cut down on "conflict of interest" concerns by holding gay married couples equally accountable.

The way current laws stand, same-sex couples are denied numerous rights while being exempted from numerous responsibilities. Conversely, heterosexual married couples are being given numerous rights and forced to comply with numerous responsibilities. How these rights and responsibilities play out from couple to couple is a real crapshoot.

Example 1

A senator's wife benefits from being able to use the Senate beauty shop free of cost. Her medical transportation is paid for by the government when she must be flown back to the States due to a serious illness while accompanying her husband on a work-related foreign trip. She receives her husband's retirement after his death.

A senator's domestic partner is denied access to all of the above.

Example 2

A female service member is killed in the line of duty. Her husband receives monthly dependency and indemnity compensation, job counseling, training, and placement services, enjoys preferences in federal employment, and may also be eligible for special life insurance and interment in a national cemetery.

A female service member is killed in the line of duty. Her domestic partner is unaware that she has died until she finds out through the woman's family. She receives none of the above benefits.

Example 3

A spouse of an ambassador to Colombia receives financial and material gifts worth thousands of dollars from a local Colombian family. Because she accepted the money and the property and did not report it, she violated the conflict of interest rules for employees and spouses of government employees. He will be terminated from his position, and both he and she will most likely go to prison.

An ambassador's same-sex domestic partner receives the same financial and material gifts. Because the two are not legally married, neither he nor his partner is held accountable for reporting them. They enjoy the extra cash and decorate their fabulous new South Beach condo!

Example 4

One member of a heterosexual couple who have been married for *two years* dies. The deceased worked 30 years for the Department of Energy. The survivor will receive the government employee's full retirement pension and Social Security benefits.

One member of a same-sex couple who have loved and cared for each other for *50 years* dies. The deceased worked for 30 years for the Department of Energy. Not a penny of the government employee's retirement pension or his 30 years of contribution to Social Security will go to his surviving domestic partner.

Example 5

A young couple is planning to buy their first home, but are strapped for cash because the wife is working and the husband is attending school. Because they are married, the amount of financial aid he receives will be limited because of *her* income. Additionally, the amount of housing loan they qualify for will necessarily take into account his student loan debt.

In the case of a domestic partnership, the two incomes

are not automatically combined and the amount of financial aid the student receives is dependent only on his own income. Additionally, the amount of his school debt will not affect the couple's housing assistance—as long as the house is purchased only in his partner's name. Once escrow closes, the student's name can be added to the paperwork.

How marriage laws—or lack thereof—affect you will be dependent on your situation and the cards life deals you. It's difficult, if not impossible, to be able to tell in advance. However, I will explore some clear ways that gay Americans are hurt by not being able to legally marry and I hope that these passages will also inspire everyone to embrace the idea of equal rights, benefits, and responsibilities in all relationships.

If You're Not Outraged, You're Not Paying Attention

Besides a variety of state rights, 1,138 federal rights come with civil marriage. For the comprehensive report by the General Accounting Office on the 1,138 rights provided by marriage, go to www.marriageequality.org.

The report mentions 13 categories in which marital status is a factor:

1) Social Security and Related Programs, Housing, and Food Stamps (82 provisions)
2) Veterans' Benefits (93 provisions)
3) Taxation (179 provisions)
4) Federal Civilian and Military Service Benefits (275 provisions)
5) Employment Benefits and Related Laws (67 provisions)

6) Immigration, Naturalization, and Aliens (42 provisions)
7) Indians (15 provisions)
8) Trade, Commerce, and Intellectual Property (44 provisions)
9) Financial Disclosure and Conflict of Interest (28 provisions)
10) Crimes and Family Violence (44 provisions)
11) Loans, Guarantees, and Payments in Agriculture (36 provisions)
12) Federal Natural Resources and Related Laws (63 provisions)
13) Miscellaneous laws (80 provisions)

Note that the largest categories are: Federal Civilian and Military Service Benefits, Veterans Benefits, and Taxation. To quote the GAO report: "The distinction between married and unmarried status is pervasive in federal tax law; this is one of the largest categories with 179 provisions."

Each state has also created its own family code and standards of what rights and responsibilities come with civil marriage. The Lambda Legal Defense and Education Fund has provided a table that summarizes the rights to be provided to registered domestic partners through the California Domestic Partner Rights and Responsibilities Act as of January 1, 2005, and compares these rights to those currently granted to married heterosexual couples in California. (Please also note that AB 205 does not provide California domestic partners with any of the 1,1138 federal rights.)

Californians, please note that these rights disappear once you set foot outside California. Once you cross the border you are officially *single* and a *legal stranger* to your domestic partner. So, don't forget that three-inch stack of paperwork, including your power of attorney, will, health directive, and domestic partnership registration form signed by the Secretary of State when you travel out of state. Stick it in your fanny pack and cart it along. In the slim chance of an emergency, it might buy you some time or possibly a sympathetic ear. Meanwhile, you may want to reconsider taking the promotion that will send you packing to Arizona, or cancel your plans to buy that winter cabin in Colorado.

To you non-Californians—don't all move here now. The housing prices are already too high and the traffic too congested as it is. Try Vermont. They have better ice cream.

An Overview of What AB 205 Will and Won't Do (With Comparisons to Civil Marriage)

Category	Right, duty, or characteristic	Provided to registered domestic partners by AB 205?	Provided by CA law to those who legally marry?
Rights and duties to one another	• Rights and duties of support during the partnership	Yes	Yes
	• Fiduciary duty between partners	Yes	Yes
	• Right not to be excluded from partner's dwelling	Yes	Yes
	• Right to damages for attempted murder	Yes	Yes
	• Rights and duties of support after termination of the partnership	Yes	Yes
	• Restriction on altering relationship by contract, except as to property	Yes	Yes
Property rights and obliga-tions	• Joint ownership of property acquired during the partnership, with rights of survivorship	Yes	Yes
	• Equal management and control of property acquired during the part-nership	Yes	Yes
	• Joint obligation for debts incurred during the partnership	Yes	Yes
	• Protection against assignment of partner's wages	Yes	Yes
	• Homestead protection against creditors of surviving partner after death of declared owner	Yes	Yes
	• Attachment of jointly owned prop-erty by creditors	Yes	Yes
	• Protection under rent control laws	Yes	Yes
	• Property interests governed by fed-eral law (such as patents and copy-rights)	**No**	Yes
	• State constitutional guarantees for protection of separate property	**No**	Yes

Category	Right, duty, or characteristic	Provided to registered domestic partners by AB 205?	Provided by CA law to those who legally marry?
Right to act on behalf of and receive informa-tion regard-ing one's partner	• Right to use any necessary force to protect partner from wrongful injury	Yes	Yes
	• Ability to request and obtain absentee ballot for partner	Yes	Yes
	• Ability to appear on behalf of part-ner in small claims court	Yes	Yes
	• Ability to defend partner's rights in certain civil actions	Yes	Yes
	• Ability to obtain notice that part-ner is being involuntarily held in mental institution	Yes	Yes
	• Ability to obtain notice that part-ner who is a parloee or probationer has certain medical conditions	Yes	Yes
Rights in judicial and other official proceed-ings	• Privilege for confidential commu-nications among partners	Yes	Yes
	• Privilege not to be forced to testify against partner	Yes	Yes
	• Right to sue for loss of consortium	Yes	Yes
	• Right to sue for violation of right of publicity of deceased partner	Yes	Yes
	• Right to sue person who provided illegal drugs to partner	Yes	Yes
	• Right to recover damages against employer liable for partner's wrongful death	Yes	Yes
Protection of the parties' children	• Presumption of parenthood regarding child born during the partnership or through alternative insemination	Yes	Yes
	• Judicial determination of custody and support of children born dur-ing the partnership	Yes	Yes
	• Ability to authorize medical treat-ment of partner's children	Yes	Yes

Category	Right, duty, or characteristic	Provided to registered domestic partners by AB 205?	Provided by CA law to those who legally marry?
Death-related matters	• Right to control disposition of remains, authorize autopsy, make anatomical gifts, and authorize exhumation	Yes	Yes
	• Right to be buried in joint or family cemetary plot	Yes	Yes
	• Identification of partner on death certificate	Yes	Yes
	• Provisions for handling inheritance after simultaneous death of partners	Yes	Yes
	• Protection of survivor's interest in joint property following partner's death	Yes	Yes
	• Protection against disinheritance by partner	Yes	Yes
	• Ability to avoid probate of jointly owned property	Yes	Yes
	• Ability of surviving partner to collect compensation provided to victims of violent crime	Yes	Yes
	• Availability of presumptions protecting interests of surviving partner under workers' compensation	Yes	Yes
Taxes	• Ability to file joint state income tax returns	**No**	Yes
	• Ability to obtain tax treatment that takes relationship into account	**Partial**	Yes
	• Exemption from transfer tax on deed or other writings transferring, dividing or allocating joint property among partners pursuant to termination of the relationship	Yes	Yes
	• Exemption from reassessment under Prop. 13 of jointly held property between partners, upon separation or termination of the relationship or after death	**No**	Yes

Category	Right, duty, or characteristic	Provided to registered domestic partners by AB 205?	Provided by CA law to those who legally marry?
Taxes (cont'd)	• Exemption from property tax on the homes of survivors of veterans who died on active duty	No	Yes
	• Partial exemption from property tax provided survivors of certain veterans	No	Yes
	• Unlimited exemptions from federal gift and estate taxes on transfers to partner	No	Yes
Licenses, permits, and franchises	• Right of franchisee to designate surviving partner to operate franchise	Yes	Yes
	• Joint interest in fishing permits	Yes	Yes
	• Ability to inherit partner's commercial fishing license	Yes	Yes
	• Ability to inherit license to run driving school	Yes	Yes
	• Ability to obtain transfer of deceased partner's special license plates	Yes	Yes
	• Ability of veteran's surviving partner to succeed on pending application for farm or home purchase	Yes	Yes
	• Partial exemption from license fee on mobile home or trailer coach owned by and constituting principal place of residence of surviving partner of veteran	Yes	Yes
Employment rights and benefits	• Right to take extended unpaid leave to care for a partner	Yes	Yes
	• State government hiring preference for surviving partners of veterans and partners of disabled veterans	Yes	Yes

Category	Right, duty, or characteristic	Provided to registered domestic partners by AB 205?	Provided by CA law to those who legally marry?
Non-tax financial matters	• Consideration of partner's income and need for support in determining student financial aid	Yes	Yes
	• Exemption of current or former partners from requirements upon transfers of real property	Yes	Yes
	• Prohibition on acceleration of mortgage on transfer to partner	Yes	Yes
	• Coverage of partner as an insured under auto insurance policies	Yes	Yes
	• Tuition fee exemption for surviving partners of veterans	Yes	Yes
	• Education assistance for surviving partners of victims of Sept. 11	Yes	Yes
	• Eligibility for Medi-Cal payments if partner is in a nursing facility	Yes	Yes
Misc. provisions	• Access to married student housing	Yes	Yes
	• Authority to use car rented by partner if licensed and of sufficient age	Yes	Yes
	• Ability to obtain overnight visitation with partners who are in prison	Yes	Yes
	• Recognition of relationship under the California Political Reform Act and Prop.34	No	Yes
Special benefits provided to public employees and their families	• Certain employees' entitlement to leave of absence after death of partner	Yes	Yes
	• Protection of partner's interest in public employee's retirement benefits and pension	Yes	Yes
	• Right to continued health coverage and benefits after death of public employee partner	Yes	Yes
	• Right of surviving partner of a deceased legislator to collect benefits	Yes	Yes
	• Right to be buried in state burial grounds if partner is a legislator	Yes	Yes

Category	Right, duty, or characteristic	Provided to registered domestic partners by AB 205?	Provided by CA law to those who legally marry?
Special benefits provided to public employees and their families (cont'd)	• Death benefits for surviving partners of firefighters and police • Scholarship for surviving partners of firefighters and peace officers • Prohibition on certain crimes against, and disclosure of residences or phone numbers of, partners of certain public officials and employees	Yes Yes Yes	Yes Yes Yes
Conflicts of interest and required disclosures	• Exclusion of gifts from partners from limitations on judges' receipt of gifts • Coverage of partners in laws governing conflicts of interest by certain government officials based on personal relationships with parties • Exclusion of interest in the income of one's partner from certain conflict of interest laws • Coverage or relationship under conflict of interest rules governing Coastal Commission members and employees	Yes Yes No No	Yes Yes Yes Yes
Discrimination protections	• Coverage under state laws prohibiting discrimination based on being or not being in the legal relationship • Coverage under federal laws prohibiting discrimination based on being or not being in the legal relationship	Yes No	Yes Yes
Entry into the institution	• Right to marry legally in California • Issuance of licenses by county clerks • Submission of certificates of registry to county clerks containing vital statistics • Solemnization by government or religious officials	No No No No	Yes Yes Yes Yes

Category	Right, duty, or characteristic	Provided to registered domestic partners by AB 205?	Provided by CA law to those who legally marry?
Termination of the partnership	• Rights and obligations relating to, and assistance in resolving disputes regarding, division of property, support, and other matters when the partners have children or significant property or debts or have been long-term registered partners	Yes	Yes
	• Requirement to file court proceedings in all cases where the relationship is being terminated	No	Yes
Rights and duties under federal law	• Rights under immigration laws	No	Yes
	• Social Security rights	No	Yes
	• Medicare rights	No	Yes
	• Rights under housing and food stamp programs	No	Yes
	• Treatment as a couple under federal tax law	No	Yes
	• Veterans' benefits	No	Yes
	• Civilian employee/military benefits	No	Yes
	• Coverage under employment benefit laws	No	Yes
	• Coverage under financial disclosure, and conflict of interest laws	No	Yes
	• Coverage under trade, commerce, and intellectual property laws	No	Yes
	• Federal agricultural loans, guarantees, and payments		
	• Rights under federal natural resources laws	No	Yes
	• Coverage under federal crimes and anti-violence laws	No	Yes
	• Treatment as a couple under Indian affairs laws	No	Yes
	• Treatment as a couple under international laws and treaties	No	Yes
Interstate treatment	• Assured recognition and guaranteed provision of rights in other jurisdictions	No	Yes
	• Recognition of out-of-state marriages as valid	No	Yes

65

Wow!

After scanning this list of rights and responsibilities, some may think that marriage is the last thing anybody should want to jump into. And they're right. Marriage *is* a lot of responsibility. It's a serious undertaking, and people need to consider carefully whether they are ready to be financially and emotionally intertwined. In fact, the marriage equality movement may inspire heterosexuals to spend more time weighing the option of marriage as well.

Whatever the drawbacks of civil marriage, the wide gap between the number of rights granted to heterosexual couples and to gay and lesbian couples is alarming. Gays and lesbians must ask themselves: Is it fair for an entire group of people to be infantilized? Is it right to be regarded in the eyes of the law as unable to take on adult responsibility and provide for our families like our non-gay counterparts? Is it not absurd to maintain that gay people don't deserve entitlement to leave of absence after the death of a partner but heterosexual people do? Or that straight firefighters' surviving partners deserve benefits but gay firefighters' surviving partners don't?

AND SPEAKING OF INJUSTICE FOR ALL...

I know there are people saying we need to heed the passages of the Bible and God's word. But if we are going back to ancient passages of the Bible to define U.S. marriage law, then why not follow the dictates of the Bible verbatim and define marriage according those as proposed in the Oakland PFLAG newsletter of September/October 2003?

1. Marriage in the United States shall consist of a union between one man and one or more women. (Gen.29, 17 28; II Sam. 3, 2-5) Marriage shall not

impede a man's right to take concubines in addition to wife or wives. (II Sam. 5:13; I Kings 11:3; II chron 11:21)

2. Marriage shall be considered valid only if the wife is a virgin. If the wife is not a virgin, she shall be executed. (Deut. 22, 13-31) Marriage of a believer and a nonbeliever shall be forbidden. (Gen. 24:3; Num 25 1-9; Ezra 9:12; Neh. 10:30)

3. Since marriage is for life, neither this constitution nor the constitution of any state nor any state or federal law shall be construed to permit divorce. (Deut. 22: 19; Mark 10:9)

4. If a married man dies without children, his brother shall marry the widow. If he refuses to marry his brother's widow or deliberately does not give her children, he shall pay a fine of one shoe and be otherwise punished in a manner to be determined by the law. (Gen. 38 6-10; Deut. 25 5-10)

Is this what they mean by following the word of God?

nine

The Power
of Ritual

*"Marriage is an Athenic weaving together of families,
of two souls with their individual fates and destinies, of
time and eternity—everyday life married to the timeless
mysteries of the soul."* —Thomas Moore, *Soul Mates*

*"Leviticus doesn't say anything about marriage. There
are many things in the Bible that Jews and Christians
don't follow. The purpose of a wedding is for people to
state publicly that this is the relationship that they are
committed to for life, and the community is there to be
supportive and celebrate the primacy of that relationship and seek God's blessings—this is Judaism, as I
know it."* —Rabbi Lisa Edwards, Congregation Beth
Chayim Chadashim, Los Angeles, CA

MARRIAGE HEEBIE-JEEBIES
The relationship of the LGBT person with religion is one
of the most difficult to negotiate. Overt discrimination by
clergy and church leaders has taken its toll on many gay
Americans, especially those raised in extremely religious
households. Is it any wonder that so many of us equate marriage with some antiquated form of human sacrifice?
Having other peoples' relationships blessed as something

holy while LGBT people are told that our own are unnatural abominations against God does not make it easy for us to embrace the idea of a church role in blessing our relationships.

But marriage isn't just about that old-time religion. The presence of a ritual establishes a ceremonial and celebratory tone, a moment that is ultimately transformative for all involved. While the rights associated with marriage are critical to the long-term cohesiveness of a couple, many consider the spiritual element of a blessing to be equally important.

Malidoma Some, shaman of the Dagara tribe of West Central Africa, emphasizes that a ritual provides the space for spiritual energies, synchronicity, fate, and perhaps even magic to appear, making the couple's ceremony an opportunity to be influenced by a greater force. "There are two parts to ritual. One part is planned. The other part cannot be planned because it is the part the Spirit is in charge of."

I'VE ALWAYS DREAMED OF A BIG CHURCH WEDDING

"We both decided to tie the knot. We knew we were going to be together for a long time. We both come from old-fashioned families and decided to have a very traditional Italian-Jewish wedding. We had about 180 guests, our parents, aunts, great aunts, as well as tons of our friends attended." —Maria and Wendy Romagnuolo

As churches, mosques, synagogues, and temples have more clergy and congregations who welcome and affirm gay members, increasing numbers of LGBT people are finding that they can express their spirituality within organized forms of religion. Younger people are less often being forced to abandon their faith when they come out because their families and other members of their religious community take a stand on their behalf.

New Jersey parent Clarice Zieja says that when she learned that her lesbian daughter, Lauren, was upset that she would never be able to legally marry, her perception of what was possible for gay people changed. "At that point, everything flip-flopped in my mind. I was programmed to think the way that everyone else did, that gay and lesbian people are different. Once my daughter said that to me, I realized that she wasn't different in any way. She wants the same things in life—to form a strong connection with one other person" (The [Washington] *Olympian*, August 2003).

According to *The Olympian*, spurred on by the momentum of town halls discussing the Lewis "Right to Marry" case in New Jersey, parents "began talking to neighbors, friends, and coworkers about why they want their gay children to be able to have the same right to a U.S. marriage license that their heterosexual children already enjoy." This dialogue then led to a PFLAG-sponsored poll that found 55% of New Jersey voters support gay marriage, compared to 41% who don't. Even more surprising was a Zogby International survey conducted from July 15 to July 19, 2003: "57 percent of New Jersey voters say their state should recognize the Canadian marriages of American gay couples."

Several New Jersey couples, with the assistance of Lambda Legal, are currently suing for the right to marry.

REVOLUTIONARY CLERGY

Black civil rights activist Rev. Cecil Williams has long been in favor of equal marriage rights. Six months after he came to Glide Memorial United Methodist Church in San Francisco, he began to perform same-sex blessings. "It was the 1960s," said Williams at the California Come Out for Equality Conference on October 11, 2003. "And it was so new. I didn't know what I was doing. I didn't know whether to call them a couple, a union, or a marriage. Sometimes I'd say 'help me' as I was marrying the people: 'What do you want me to say?' Some of them didn't know themselves." Reverend Williams now calls all such blessings marriages, reasoning that only marriage can provide LGBT people with the full dignity they deserve.

Several ministers have defied their church's official position on same-sex marriage. In January 1999, an act of revolt occurred in Sacramento, California, when 68 Methodist ministers co-officiated at a holy union ceremony for two lesbians. Charges were filed against the ministers, but the case was dismissed and the charges dropped against Rev. Don Fado, whose church had hosted the holy union. When Omaha-based Rev. Jimmy Creech chose to support full equality for same-sex couples by offering blessings, he was defrocked by the Methodist Church in November 1999. Another Methodist Minister, Rev. Gregory Dell, violated Methodist law when he performed a holy union ceremony between two gay parishioners. He was advised that he could sign a pledge vowing that he would no longer perform same-sex marriage ceremonies or be defrocked. Dell declined to sign the pledge and was suspended indefinitely in 1999.

> ### *"Marriage—anything less is less than equal. I will not accept anything that is less than equal."*
> ### —Rev. Cecil Williams

Stephen Van Kuiken, a minister from Ohio, was found guilty on April 21, 2003 of violating the constitution of the Presbyterian Church (USA) by marrying same-sex couples. (Although a denominational court ruled in 2000 that Presbyterian ministers may *bless* same-sex unions, they may not *marry* the couples.) Yet Van Kuiken continues to do so because he believes "same-sex marriages are Christian unions."

Because of punitive actions by the church in these and other well-known cases, many ministers are afraid to perform same-sex blessings but have found other ways to make their support of same-sex couples known. In 2003 a Connecticut group of pro-marriage equality clergy from the Unitarian Universalist Association, Presbyterian Church (USA), Reform Judaism, and the United Church of Christ refused to sign marriage licenses for heterosexuals. The rationale: If one is officiating for marriages, one is complicit in the unfairness of the law.

> *"The only way I know how to stop participating in the bias is to stop participating in the legal dimension of it."*
> **—Rev. Kathleen McTigue, senior minister, Unitarian Society of New Haven**

In July 2003, Rev. Phil Campbell, senior pastor of Park Hill Congregational United Church of Christ in Denver, founded the Colorado Clergy for Equality in Marriage because of his belief that "gay men and lesbians are entitled to the same right to marry—in a marriage of love, mutuality, and respect—that is available to my wife and me as a heterosexual couple." Groups like Colorado Clergy for Equality in Marriage have also been founded in Massachusetts and California.

"History, I believe, will view legislation against same-sex marriage as being insensitive, invalid, and

illogical, as was the legislation that prohibited inter-racial marriage." —Rev. Gilbert Caldwell, retired United Methodist Minister

Other clergy have the support of their leadership and joyfully participate in the ceremonial marriages of same-sex couples. Rabbi Lisa Edwards, of Congregation Beth Chayim Chadashim (BCC) in Los Angeles, blesses six to 10 same-sex marriages per year. Since 1994 she has per-formed as many as 90 weddings. "Reconstructionist, Renewal, and Reform Judaism all support same-sex mar-riage," notes Rabbi Edwards. "And as a movement, con-servatives don't, but many conservative rabbis do." When asked if she sees a difference between same-sex and differ-ent-sex couples she adds, "I don't see a difference in the commitment of same-sex couples. I do think, though, that same-sex couples are under the scrutiny of others who believe their relationships won't last."

THE BONDS OF LOVE

While it's clear that marriage transforms a relationship, it must also be noted that each action taken in preparation for a wedding weaves the couple closer together, culminating with their vows. Rabbi Edwards explains, "Often a couple doesn't realize the depth of their wedding. At first, it's a polit-ical statement, a celebration, or a party, but after the plan-ning of the ceremony they see their relationship in a deeper way. A wedding publicizes and ritualizes a commitment a couple has to one another. By the time a person is standing under the chuppah, they have already made many commit-ments. They've examined their relationship more carefully."

TRANSFORMATION OF FAMILY

A marriage ceremony puts the same-sex relationship

into a language and context everyone is familiar with and has the potential to transform what the couple means to each other in the eyes of family members, friends, and coworkers. By participating in this public step, parents of gay and lesbian couples are more easily able to calculate how long their children have been together and acknowledge each anniversary with them.

> *"It was nice to see all of my daughter's and her partner's friends. It was phenomenal to have so many people there celebrating the girls' love."* —Jan Duchon, Gresham, Oregon

A marriage ceremony can also help a family come out and come to terms with their child's sexual orientation in a positive setting. Rabbi Edwards has seen this many times. "It's really powerful to watch reluctant or distressed parents witnessing their child's same-sex marriage and to see their attitudes change during the course of a ceremony. There's a lot of fear and embarrassment, and then watching them lighten up—going from not looking at the couple, not looking up—and then they begin to notice what's going on and you see their physiology change, they lighten up and they actually transform to smiling."

Gretchen Hamm describes understanding her daughter's same-sex marriage as a process. "Every mother dreams of the ideal wedding for her daughter, and I am no different. I have always envisioned a wedding where my daughter marries her beloved: someone who loves her and cares for her. Of course, I must admit that I had originally envisioned a man standing at her side, representing those things. But as you know, life is full of surprises sometimes!" As plans for Hamm's daughter's 1999 wedding began to unfold, she saw how susceptible she was to thinking of a lesbian wedding as not quite real. Taking herself to task, she set herself a standard: Her actions as the "mother of *a* bride" must be the same as if she were the "mother of *the* bride." Hamm tried to remain conscious of her biases and constantly asked herself, *What would I do if she were marrying a man?* This inquiry led to her willingness to "approach this wedding with the same legitimacy, reverence, and excitement that the institution of heterosexual marriage typically receives."

> *"Do what you do best: Follow your hearts, make a commitment to love and honor each other no matter what anyone else has to say. As far as I'm concerned, you can call your union "mother-approved" while we celebrate love and wait on those politicians to catch up with us."* —Gretchen Hamm, creator of Twobrides.com and Twogrooms.com

For those who do not have the support of their families of origin, a wedding ceremony might reawaken old wounds, but the support of friends and community members has the potential to be healing. While the absence of certain family members presents a challenge, it can also allow us to define "family" in ways that make sense, releasing us from the usual cookie-cutter expectations. Creating new rituals that incorporate close friends and family-of-choice is a great way to overcome this pain. Supportive members of the community bearing witness to the ceremony will help strengthen a couple's bond.

THE VALUE OF PLANNING, DOCUMENTING, AND ANNOUNCING

Even the simple act of *planning* a wedding is a way to deepen your connection. Constructing a ceremony, set-

Release Yourself From Cookie-Cutter Expectations

"My family was less supportive than Ed's and opted not to attend. However, all of Ed's family attended and admitted that it was one of the best weddings they had ever gone to. Also, the support of our friends, coworkers, and neighbors made our entire ceremony and reception so much more memorable." —Michael Del Rosso-Steffan, New Jersey (*Gay Parent* magazine, May-June 2003)

ting the tone, creating a shared vision, and writing your own vows aren't easy things to do, but a couple can learn a lot about themselves just by going through the process. For Molly and me, the planning process fleshed out our sense of common values and of the symbols that embodied who we were as a couple. It set the stage for what a life together may look like in the years to come. Working together to create that magical day or night can solidify a relationship even before the vows are formally exchanged.

Documenting the ceremony with photos and video provide a place to return to when a couple needs to recapture the joy and magic of the commitment—an especially valuable tool when caught up with bills, obligations, and other "worses" of the "for better or worse" vow. Sometimes sending a video to a family member who has chosen not to attend can help him or her accept the reality in a way that may be less threatening.

"One person watched the video of his son's wedding and wrote him that he was sorry he hadn't attended, because he hadn't realized how important it was to his son and the depth of their commitment."
—Rabbi Lisa Edwards, Congregation Beth Chayim Chadashim, Los Angeles, Calif.

In August 2002, *The New York Times* announced that it would begin running same-sex civil union notices. At the time more than 70 newspapers were already running announcements for same-sex commitment ceremonies. And by December 20, 2002, 180 newspapers were following suit, including the *Southern Utah News*, *The Boston Globe*, and the *Los Angeles Times*.

The New York Times seems to have normalized the whole process—including civil unions and partnership registrations—as demonstrated in this explanation on its Web page titled "How to Submit an Announcement":

> In the case of a wedding, a civil union or a partnership registration, we must have the name of the person who will sign the official certificate. Please give the exact title and affiliation. For an interfaith event, please include the names and affiliations of any other officiants who will participate. Please also state the exact location of the event.

On January 20, 2003, the Montana *Missoulian* joined the list when Kara Hagen and Heidi Bates submitted their ceremony announcement. But the lesbian couple first had to reassure the editor when he called to make sure the whole thing wasn't a prank. "We're doing it because we're getting married, and we want the world to know." Bates felt that it was important for them to announce their wedding and to call it a marriage "because, for me, that's what it was and that's what it is."

> ### *"I think it is tacky. It is pretending it is a marriage, and it isn't."*
> ### —Phyllis Schlafy, Eagle Forum president

Now that these means of recognizing same-sex relationships exist, I strongly encourage gay and lesbian couples to take advantage of them. If you must skip the marriage equality rally or the marriage license request-protest, be sure to submit your wedding announcement or anniversary picture to the newspaper.

And if you haven't yet participated in or been to a same-sex marriage ceremony, put it on the top of your annual goals to get invited to one. You'll be so glad you did.

ten

Community Recognition

"If you study the California Code with regard to marriage, you'll get 4,000 hits where spousal status makes a difference."
—Toni Broaddus, J.D., Equality California

SCENE 1: UNITED STATES

Imagine you and your sweetie are traveling. After a long day in the car or on the plane you check into your hotel. The bellhop takes your bags to your room, opens the door, and *voilà* there they are: the two twin beds. Your partner clears his throat. Which one of you is going to take the elevator back downstairs to ask for the double bed? Or are you just going to squeeze into one of the twin beds, get a terrible night's sleep, and in the morning muss the sheets to avoid the awkwardness of the whole situation?

You flip a coin and lose. You take a deep breath, approach the counter and address the confused receptionist.

"You want a double bed?" echoes through the lobby. "But you're both men."

You hand her back the key and explain awkwardly that yes, you are both men but you still want a double bed. She begins to have that "A-ha!" expression as she slowly exchanges your key and raises one eyebrow. You quickly make your way back to the elevator, retrieve your partner, luggage, pride, and what's left of your dignity trailing somewhere far behind you. Cut!

Scene 2: Canada

Now imagine another scenario in which the same awkward situation plays out, but now you have leverage. When you walk downstairs this time, you feel sure of yourself because now you can make it clear to the receptionist that the two of you are married. Your relationship is clear, justified, and legal.

Scene 3: Back in the United States

You call up the dentist's office to schedule a cleaning for you and your love muffin. (Due to her dentist-phobia, she's at risk of going AWOL if you aren't there to make sure she gets those pearlies polished.) After you schedule your appointment, you begin to schedule hers. There is an awkward moment where the receptionist insinuates that she will have to call for herself. Wouldn't it be so much easier if you could just say: "I also need to schedule a cleaning for my wife." It's more to the point and yes, maybe there will still be that awkward silence after you give them your wife's name, but at least they are clear on the concept. When you are married, even if it is only in Canada, it makes it more comfortable for you to use the terms *husband* or *wife*, or *spouse* without cognitive dissonance.

Unfortunately, in the United States, people can choose not to take us seriously (except for a few states in which we have minimal protections that afford us minimal respect). The average citizen, corporation, and government official can give us just as much consideration and respect as "domestic partnerships" dictates to them. In other words, we are still "playing house," having "pretend families," and "make-believe ceremonies," while our heterosexual friends, family members, and coworkers are having "real marriages," "real weddings," and "real families."

"In California we went from being legal strangers to next of kin, but we are still a long way from being legal spouses."
—Toni Broaddus, Equality California

The Second-Class Status of Gay Americans

In Washington State, Tom Butts and Scott Carter dropped off the invitations for their upcoming wedding in Canada at Starfish Creative, a Seattle printer. The owner, Patty Pauls, refused to take their business, stating that she was against marriages between people of the same sex. Luckily for Tom and Scott, they knew about a Seattle nondiscrimination law that prohibits businesses from discriminating based on sexual orientation. The couple is now pursuing legal action against Pauls. Nevertheless, because same-sex marriage is not legal in the United States, many Americans not only feel comfortable treating Tom and Scott like second-class citizens, they'd be supported by their governments in doing so. The attitude is much like that of a white-owned Southern lunch counter in the early 1960s that righteously refused to serve African-American customers.

eleven

Employment

"Sixty-two percent of heterosexuals believe that employees with same-sex partners should be equally eligible for key workplace benefits available to spouses of married employees." —Witeck-Combs and Harris interactive poll, October 2003

THE EXPLOITABLE MINORITY

Imagine a CEO brainstorming with his inner circle about ways to cut costs.

"I've got an idea!" one offers. "We hire more gay people!"

"What?" the enraged boss yells out. "Why would we want to do that?"

"Because, boss, gays work harder than their heterosexual counterparts because they are always afraid you are going to fire them for being gay. We don't have to pay any spousal benefits like health insurance and leave, and no death benefits when they die. Over time, we'll save lots of money, and we'll look progressive because we respect diversity!"

"Brilliant!"

"Yes, and they are less likely to have kids, and if their same-sex partner has kids, we don't have to acknowledge that they are theirs, so no loss of productivity and hiring temps to deal with maternity or paternity leaves. Just think of all the money we'd save from not having to provide them with benefits."

Whether the discrimination is conscious or by default, we offer employers financial breaks because they do not have to provide for our families and they don't have to feel bad about discriminating against us because the law fully supports it. We are an exploitable minority, especially when we are in the closet. Who better to ask to cover the holiday on call than the "single" guy or gal who is too closeted to admit he promised to visit his partner's family or too afraid to come out to his gay joke-cracking boss because there still are no employment protections for LGBT people? In fact, sometimes we don't even have to be closeted for bosses or coworkers to make the assumption that we should work holidays because often they do not recognize our families as family.

There are numerous situations where same-sex couples are denied equal opportunity to use sick leave and family leave to care for their loved ones. Jeff hurts his back moving into his new home with his long-term partner Pedro and is unable to care for himself. Pedro calls in sick to work and tells his boss that he must take Jeff to a doctor's appointment because Jeff is unable to drive. Pedro's boss informs him that he cannot use his sick leave to care for Jeff. Pedro points out that earlier that month coworker Marsha was able to stay home when her husband was ill. His boss informs him that sick leave is only allowed for family members, and Jeff is not considered his family member. She says she is sorry, but that is the company policy. He is welcome to use vacation leave or take nonpaid leave.

Maxine is diagnosed with breast cancer and begins to undergo chemotherapy treatments. The process is draining, and she is unable to care for her most basic needs.

Maxine's partner, Donna, approaches her boss, who's sympathetic to Donna's concern for Maxine, but falls short of allowing her extended unpaid leave to care for her, something Donna's coworker Evan was able to do when his wife was sick with Hepatitis C. The sympathetic boss acknowledges similarities between the two situations, but states that his hands are tied because the policy recognizes only *married*, not simply *cohabiting* couples.

LGBT people in Vermont, California, and Hawaii should thank the lawmakers who helped begin to level the playing field. In these states, LGBT citizens are allowed to use family leave to care for a partner. Additionally, Pres. Bill Clinton, despite many of his shortcomings and unfulfilled promises, acted like a true friend when he extended benefits to LGBT civilian federal employees with the 1993 Family and Medical Leave Act. This landmark measure provided LGBT federal employees an opportunity to take leave to care for a loved one who was "like family or as close as family." But even with the passage of this act, LGBT federal employees are still discriminated against because either they or their supervisors do not know about or understand it.

As a federal employee myself, I've seen the truth of this first-hand. One of my coworkers was told she'd be considered AWOL if she didn't leave her recently hospitalized partner and "Get back to work!" For just this reason, I keep a copy of this bill in my desk drawer next to my bimonthly time sheets in case I need to pull it out and show it to a new boss or to photocopy it for a disbelieving coworker who's afraid to turn in a leave slip without a highlighted copy of the act attached. Without federal recognition of our marriages it is far too easy for non-gay people to believe they can completely overlook the significance of our relationships and treat our partners as nothing more than friends or legal strangers.

"Marriage Lite" States and Private Companies

Gay and lesbian Americans are denied access to the employment benefits their coworkers enjoy. Marriage allows heterosexual employees the right to bereavement leave, sick leave, health insurance benefits, life insurance, adoption assistance, disability benefits, and support to one spouse when the other spouse is relocated for work. When progressive employers such as Nike, Ford Motor Company, Starbucks (or any other of the 198 gay-friendly Fortune 500s) provide domestic partner benefits such as group health insurance coverage, the employee is taxed by the U.S. government for this "special benefit." Heterosexual married couples are not.

Some businesses also provide additional benefits related to the products and/or services they supply. As noted in *The Advocate*'s October 14, 2003 issue, which evaluated the top U.S. Companies that offer domestic partner benefits, Bausch and Lomb allows employees' domestic partners access to "free contact lenses and membership in the company's fitness center." Hyatt Hotels allows employees' domestic partners to receive employee rates for hotel stays.

Sadly, there are many companies who do not provide these types of benefits to registered same-sex partners. During the Exxon-Mobil merger, Mobil employees went from having domestic partner benefits to losing them. Can you imagine if, after a merger, straight employees were told that they would no longer have spousal benefits? The union would have wiped up the floor with the corporate high brass. But, hey, it's easy to save a few bucks at the expense of the queers.

As we celebrate companies like Borders Books, AOL Time Warner, and Metropolitan Life Insurance that already provide domestic partner benefits, it's important to understand that these benefits are not on par with spousal benefits and can be lost at any time.

SOME OF MY BEST FRIENDS ARE
DEA AND IRS AGENTS

Yes, some of your queer friends do work for Uncle Sam in a nonmilitary capacity—and they are being discriminated against. After all, the U.S. government is the biggest American employer, and it doesn't offer domestic partner benefits, lagging behind the several thousand firms in the private sector, including many Fortune 500 companies, that do.

Maybe you didn't want to grow up and audit people's taxes or kick in drug dealers' doors, but some queers did, and they deserve the same rights and benefits as their heterosexual peers. Frankly, I didn't expect to be providing psychological counseling for a federal agency, but I've been doing it for seven years now and don't plan on going anywhere any time soon.

Of course, there are times when the private sector beckons. When I learn of positions in the private sector that offer such domestic partner benefits as health care, I add up how much Molly and I would save if I could put her on my health plan. I find it particularly frustrating that I can't make her the beneficiary of my pension in case of my death. I have coworkers who have been married more than once over the course of the seven years I've been on the job, and each new spouse has access to pension benefits in case of the partner's death.

GOING POSTAL

Several years ago I heard a guy from the post office talking about being on a flight with a coworker headed to a training seminar. The guy was gay and had been in a relationship with his partner for 20 years; the other, a newly-married heterosexual man. During the flight, there was a bout of severe turbulence, and as the two sat praying, hoping that they would see their loved ones again, the newlywed expressed his relief that if he were to die his wife would get his pension. The gay man clutched his armrest, enraged that his partner of 20 years would be treated as a legal stranger and nothing more. The stark contrast motivated him to begin speaking out for *national* domestic partnership benefits, which to this day do not exist. He got my attention, though.

And I hope I'm getting yours.

THE DOMESTIC PARTNERSHIP BENEFITS AND OBLIGATIONS ACT (DPBO)

"It's time for the federal government to follow the lead of 11 state governments, over 150 local governments, and more than 5,000 private-sector employers and recognize that providing benefits to domestic partners is not just the fair thing to do, it's good business. Corporations are not required to do this in most places. They do it because it helps attract high quality employees." —Rep. Barney Frank

On June 12, 2003, Minnesota senator Mark Dayton reintroduced the Domestic Partnership Benefits and Obligations Act (DPBO), S. 1252, in the Senate. Since 1997, Massachusetts representative Barney Frank has sponsored HR 2426, the House version of the bill. DPBO would provide the domestic partner of a federal employee the same benefits as a spouse of a federal employee. According to a posting on Frank's Web site, the DPBO would include benefits to domestic partners such as "retirement benefits, life insurance, health insurance, and compensation for work-related injuries." This bill also amended the Internal Revenue Code to extend the tax exemption for employer contributions to accident and health plans to domestic partners. Frank points out that "at a time when there is a substantial salary gap between government and private-sector employers with similar jobs, it simply makes sense to add a low cost benefit to help attract more qualified people to the federal government, and make it easier to retain them once they start work."

It would be great if more representatives could be as fair-minded as Frank. At present there are only 89 cosponsors in the House and nine in the Senate. (Note to Californians: Senator Feinstein has not yet agreed to cosponsor the bill, although Senator Boxer has.) See Appendix E for how you can make a difference in contacting your senators and representatives to urge them to support this important legislation.

Many of the 2004 Democratic presidential candidates—Sharpton, Dean, Gephardt, Lieberman, Kucinich, and Kerry—support this bill. In fact, Kerry and Lieberman signed on as cosponsors when Dayton reintroduced the bill to the Senate on June 12, 2003.

"There is simply no good reason to discriminate among employees in committed relationships: Equal work should mean equal pay—and benefits."
—Rep. Barney Frank

Another bill designed to level the workplace playing field is the Tax Equity for Health Plan Beneficiaries Act (HR 935). This bill would stop taxing employees for the benefit of providing health care to their domestic partners. This bill, introduced by Washington Democratic representative Jim McDermott, has 74 cosponsors. Unfortunately, neither HR 935 or HR 2426 has much of a chance of being heard under the current speaker of the House, Tom Delay. Nothing will happen unless LGBT people and their allies start to shake things up a bit and create a loud, unstoppable voice demanding full equality and uncompromised access to civil marriage.

twelve

Nine Common
Arguments Against
Marriage Equality

To date, lawsuits to allow same-sex couples the freedom to marry have been filed in 15 states and the District of Columbia. Among them are:

Baker v. Nelson (Minnesota, 1971)
Singer v. Hara (Washington, 1971)
Berkett v. the county clerk (Wisconsin, 1971)
Jones v. Hallahan (Kentucky, 1973)
Thorton v. Timmers (Ohio, 1974)
Adams v. Howerton (Colorado, 1975)
Dean v. D.C. (District of Columbia, 1990)
Fullington v. Ohio (1990)
Baehr v. Lewin (Hawaii, 1993)
Baehr v. Miike (1996)
Baehr v. Anderson (Hawaii, 1998)
Cable-McCarthy v. California (California, 1993)
Underwood v. Florida (Florida, 1993)
Callender v. Corbett (Arizona, 1994)
Brause v. Alaska (Alaska, 1998)
Storrs v. Holcomb (New York, 1996)
Baker v. State of Vermont (Vermont, 1998)
Goodridge v. Dept. of Public Health (Massachusetts, 2001)

Lewis et. al. v. Harris et. al. (New Jersey, 2002)
Morrison et. al. v. O' Bannon (Indiana, 2002)
Standhardt v. Superior Court (Arizona, 2003)

In the first case ever filed, *Baker v. Nelson* (Minnesota, 1971), the couple argued that denying them the right to marry was unconstitutional because it denied them their 9th and 14th Amendment rights to liberty and property without due process and equal protection under the law. The denial of their case was based on the following arguments: a) marriage is a union between a man and a woman; b) marriage is for procreation; and c) marriage is for the rearing of children. These arguments, along with six others commonly used to defend the denial of equal marriage rights to gays and lesbians are listed below (with rebuttals):

1. "Marriage is for procreation!"

Well, gay people do procreate and raise children—and many heterosexual couples do not.

The last U.S. census found that one quarter of all gay male and a third of all lesbian households were raising children. Even more LGBT people would contemplate raising children if they had legal protections for their families and wouldn't have to contend with state laws making it illegal for them to adopt or to become foster parents. The laws of four states (Utah, Arkansas, Mississippi, and Florida) explicitly prohibit gays and lesbians from adopting children or serving as foster parents. In 2003 the North Dakota legislature passed a bill denying foster parent and adoption rights to LGBT people. Similar bills were introduced in Iowa, Oklahoma, and Texas but have not passed.

If marriage is for procreation only, what about the numerous childless heterosexual marriages? What about a man who wishes to marry a post-menopausal woman? What about a woman who marries a man who's had a vasectomy? Should these marriages be annulled? Furthermore, should marriages between infertile heterosexuals be outlawed altogether? Why is it that one group of Americans can be denied marriage rights when they actually *can* produce a biological child, yet other nonprocreating pairs can have access to numerous rights, benefits, and protections?

2. "If civil marriage was legal to same-sex partners, then religious institutions would be forced into performing ceremonies."

God forbid!

It's unlikely that religious institutions would be forced into doing anything. That's where separation of church and state come in. Hmm, how does that work? The state can't force the church into doing things, but the church can dictate to American politicians to turn a blind eye to the constitution for the sake of "morality." Besides, there are already many clergy performing same-sex blessings, unions, and religious marriages. And these freedom fighters are being sued, kicked out of their churches, and ridiculed for their commitment to justice and equality—for living their faith.

3. "Marriage has always been between a man and a woman."

This sounds more like a temper tantrum than an argument. It's purely emotional. "Marriage has always been between a man and a woman." And?! Times change, folks. In this country, white men were once the only people who could vote, women were the property of their husbands, and African-Americans were slaves. Just because we have always done something a certain way doesn't mean it's right!

4. "Same-sex marriage would threaten the institution of marriage."
Come on now. How is this really possible?

Powerful enough to tear down the institution of marriage with a single vow!

What about poverty, lack of education, divorce, infidelity, and domestic violence? What about the prevalent mentality of "throw away and move on to the next one if this one doesn't work"? These couldn't possibly be the reasons that heterosexual marriages are failing. The real cause has to be those infernal gay people! *Queer Eye*'s Fabulous Five pointing out the flaws of the helpless straight guy who is forced to alter his appearance to live up to some gay standard of style or risk losing his girlfriend or wife. Lesbians brainwashing their heterosexual girlfriends with the tenants of feminism! Yes, those gay people modeling their egalitarian relationships where the housework is shared and the relationship is based on love, not obligation and hundreds of years of traditional oppression would definitely threaten the institution of marriage.

How could marriage be any more threatened than it already is? Gay people might actually bring some dignity back into the picture.

5. "Same-sex marriage will lead to the decline of Western Civilization."
Righhhhhht! I'm telling you, there is no bigger threat to society than gay men, lesbians, and transsexual individuals seeking equal relationship rights. The war in

Iraq, terrorism, investment fund scandals, unemployment, poverty, domestic violence, the war on drugs, teen pregnancy, and the high crime rate are nothing compared to the threat same-sex marriage poses to the moral fiber of Western civilization. It sounds funny, but it's not, when you realize that there really are people who believe this propaganda, and politicians like George W. Bush who are using this issue to get re-elected. (See:"Marriage Protection Week," pages 112–115).

Somehow if you start giving marriage rights to gay people, then heterosexuals aren't going to want to play anymore. "I don't want to get married now that gay people can do it. It's not special anymore." If this happens, children will be born out of wedlock and raised in single-parent homes.

Wait a minute, this has already happened!

It's legal for a man to marry...

* his first cousin (in 20 out of 50 states)
* his ex-lover's adopted daughter (as did Woody Allen)
* Britney Spears, or any other single gal he hardly knows, on a spontaneous visit to Las Vegas
* the day after his divorce is final
* the second his 20th divorce is final
* even if he's impotent
* at the age of 100 (and to leave his estate tax-free to his 18-year-old wife!)
* if he's in prison for rape, multiple murders, child molestation, kidnapping, or corporate scandal
* another man in Texas (as long as that man is a female-to-male transsexual)

6. "Same-sex marriage is a special right granted to gays. Straight people aren't asking for special rights to marry people of the same sex. Why should gay people be able to marry people of the same sex?"

This one is just absurd. The right to marry the person of one's choice is a fundamental, constitutional right. LGBT people are not asking for special rights; we simply want to exercise our constitutional right to "liberty, justice, and the pursuit of happiness." It's unfair to willfully discriminate against us by creating special laws and amendments to the Constitution in order to deny us rights that others enjoy.

7. "Marriage opens the gates to legalizing incest, polygamy, and bestial marriage."

While the acceptance of marriage equality may give some extremists fodder for their arguments for polygamy, incest, or bestiality, I think most people will recognize the difference between two loving adults wanting to share a lifetime commitment and Old McDonald wanting to tie the knot with his chickens, his cow, or all five of his sisters.

Still, I can't tell you how often I hear opponents of marriage equality tell me that if the law changed and I was able to marry Molly, what would keep people from creating laws that would allow them to marry their dogs? I hear these arguments so much, it makes me wonder why these guys are always thinking about marrying their dogs and if there is another meaning to "a dog is man's best friend." Personally, I'm not especially worried that my elected officials are going to run out and pass laws allowing people to marry animals. And I'm still not clear how bestial marriage would provide any benefits to either party.

8. "Homosexuality is immoral!"

Divorce, contraception, fertility therapy, a belief that

the earth revolves around the sun, interracial marriage, women in the workplace, and even left-handedness have all been deemed immoral at one point or another by the church. Imagine what America would look like if the Pope was running the country instead of a president elected by the democratic process (or not, as the case may currently be).

Just because the church feels a certain way doesn't mean that everyone else in this country has to change their ways to follow those beliefs. The separation of church and state in this country, means that one group's morality isn't pushed on another's. But same-sex marriage seems to be an exception: Even the current president feels he can use his faith-based discrimination to codify the definition of marriage as between one man and one woman.

9. "Marriage is a sacred institution that will lose its tradition if gays can marry."

Marriage is an institution that has changed over time, and each time it has changed, there have been fanatics who have predicted the demise of the institution and society. In the 1800s, slaves were denied the right to marry and engaged in a ritual that we might consider similar to modern-day commitment ceremonies: They jumped a broom, a ritual that finalized marriage in all but the legal sense, denying them all state and federal rights. Granting slaves the right to legally marry would have jeopardized slavery as an institution. From 1938 to the 1960s, the institution of marriage was perceived to be under attack, as was the entire moral fiber of civilization, at least according to a majority of bigots who at the time lashed out violently against interracial marriage and equal rights for blacks and other ethnic minorities. Opponents stated it was because they didn't want the two races to mix, but the races had been mixing for years, beginning with the rape of black women by white slaveowners. In addition, if marriage were allowed between two people of different races, it meant the races could be considered equal, something that flew in the face of white supremacy—much like how heterosexism and the assignation of moral inferiority to gay and lesbian Americans is used to justify the withholding of basic human rights such as employment, housing, and marital opportunities.

Just because there are fewer of us does not mean we are insane, deviant, criminal, or sinners. Yet, LGBT people have had to fight hard to overcome these labels. In 1973, the American Psychiatric Association removed homosexuality from its list of mental disorders. The U.S. Supreme Court finally overturned the sodomy laws in 2003. Our next frontier lies within the temples, churches, synagogues, and mosques. It is in these houses of worship that we must fight to prove we are citizens, not sinners. It is the last roadblock to our full citizenship, to our freedom and equality.

thirteen

Resistance in the Gay and
Lesbian Community

*"One hot summer's day a Fox was strolling through
an orchard till he came to a bunch of Grapes just
ripening on a vine which had been trained over a
lofty branch. 'Just the thing to quench my thirst,'
quoth he. Drawing back a few paces, he took a run
and a jump, and just missed the bunch. Turning
round again with a One, Two, Three, he jumped up,
but with no greater success. Again and again he tried
after the tempting morsel, but at last had to give it
up, and walked away with 'I am sure they are sour.'
It is easy to despise what you cannot get."*
—Aesop, "The Fox and the Grapes"

When talking to people about marriage equality, I
cannot tell you the number of times I've heard these three
words in response: "Marriage is Heterosexist!" And with
those three words, many LGBT and LGBT-friendly people write off the institution and all the rights that come
with it as superfluous, unnecessary, and unworthy of
their time and energy.

This argument might deserve a morsel of credibility,
but the obvious counter is that anything can be viewed as

heterosexist. Reproduction is heterosexist. The human body's plumbing is heterosexist. Even partner dancing is heterosexist—one person leads and the other follows. And most mainstream movies are heterosexist. But do we stop going to the movies and renting videos in protest? Hardly! Since we aren't going to refuse to go to the movies or to take swing or salsa lessons because of the inherent heterosexism involved, why do we choose to sacrifice over 1,138 rights and protections? Why limit ourselves and our families from having full equality and dignity?

Many of the amazing people working to legalize same-sex marriage today also once viewed the institution of marriage as outmoded and, yes, heterosexist. Being marginalized manifests itself in many interesting ways, including becoming comfortable settling for less. Like Aesop's fox, many of us have concocted reasons why marriage would sour our palettes, just to take the sting out of being denied the right to partake. Others become too Bohemian to want the rights afforded everyone else in society. It's hip to be the rejected outsider.

But it doesn't really matter what LGBT people think of marriage, because right now they're barred from truly making a choice. They have no right to *choose* whether they believe in marriage or not, because for gays and lesbians, the state—and even some of their closest political allies—say that what they want doesn't matter.

Think of all the lesbians who gave up penetration and sex toys in the '70s because it was heterosexist. How many now own merchandise from Good Vibrations—and wonder why they waited so long?

Marriage is the same way.

If you think about it, what is *more* heterosexist?

(Hint: You do not need to be good at multiple-choice quizzes to answer correctly.)

A. Same-sex couples and transsexual individuals being denied 1,138 federal rights and a plethora of state rights that heterosexual couples have access to through civil marriage.

or

B. Same-sex couples and transsexual individuals receiving the 1,138 federal rights and a plethora of state rights that heterosexual couples have access to through civil marriage.

IF YOU DON'T WANT A MARRIAGE, DON'T HAVE ONE!

It's really simple. I don't want to hunt, serve in the military, become a Mormon, or get an abortion, but some people do! And gosh darn it, this is America, where people are supposed to have rights and freedom, and where we believe in liberty, justice, and the pursuit of happiness.

The issue really is about freedom of choice for all people. I don't personally practice Mormonism, but my cousin Nick does; and I would fight for his right to practice his religion, as I would for any other person who was being discriminated against. Why? Because this country is built on the separation of church and state and I, like most Americans, believe that all people should have equal access to civil liberties, rights, and freedoms.

Even if marriage is not for you, is it fair that your gay and lesbian friends are being discriminated against?

100

"And if somebody said that gays couldn't have hunting licenses, I'd be out there fighting for the right of gays and lesbians to carry guns and hunt. And then, after all gays and lesbians had access to hunting licenses, I'd work to eradicate hunting." —Beth Robinson, civil rights attorney

MARRIAGE IS GAY LIBERATION!

I've been a gay activist since 1985. Sadly, I missed the heyday of the '70s Gay Liberation Movement, but I have profited from the courage and hard work of those who came before me. I understand that a large part of the movement was about sexual freedom and the right to express oneself fully. And I am also familiar with the idea that fighting for equal marriage rights is antithetical to the movement, that it would assimilate queer people into mainstream society, force them to live a straight reality, and render them invisible.

While I understand the nature of these arguments, I have to ask: What could be more liberating than having full access to an institution that has been denied us? What could be more liberating than to achieve a place in society that the religious right is vehemently fighting to keep us from? In a September issue of *The Village Voice*, ("The Radical Case for Gay Marriage: why progressives must join this fight") Richard Goldstein stated that "if the Right succeeds in barring gay marriage, the fall-out will do much more to set back sexual freedom than any wedding vow."

Another argument I often hear is that marriage is an issue for an elite gay fringe. This couldn't be farther from the truth, as Goldstein succinctly noted: "There are many more poor queer families than meets the media's eye, and they are the ones who stand to gain the most from marriage rights." Goldstein also noted that 34 percent of lesbian and gay couples in the South were raising kids, many of them lesbians of color who were deprived of the marriage-associated legal protections such as being able to qualify for public housing, health insurance benefits, or the right to make medical decisions for each other and their children.

Many progressives fail to see the connection between marriage rights and queer poverty.

MARRIAGE IS ONE OF THE LAST FRONTIERS FOR GAY FREEDOM FIGHTERS

Jerry Falwell's number one declared goal for 2003-2004 is to encourage Congress to pass the Federal Marriage Amendment to ensure that LGBT people are barred from being able to legally marry under the U.S. Constitution. Marriage is where the gay liberation movement needs to be right now. While we are out being liberated in bars, pride parades, and in between the sheets, the religious right is ensuring our second-class citizenship. It's time to get clear on what the real issues are.

Gay marriage is gay liberation!

The religious right is not trying to make gays conform through marriage. They are not interested in encouraging us to settle down and be monogamous. If they were, this would be a culture war between the don't-fence-us-in kind and the marrying kind. The religious right does not truly care about LGBT sexual freedom or how many people we have sex with or how many STDs we get. What they care about is gays and lesbians infiltrating the sacred institution of marriage, and thus legitimizing same-sex love. Think about it: When was the last time you saw a far right religious group fighting for gays to be monogamous? What they *really* care about is that gays and lesbians could become full and equal citizens under the law.

According to a National Gay and Lesbian Task Force report, the Concerned Women for America recently warned that same-sex marriage "poses a new threat to U.S. border security." The organization called a legally married Canadian same-sex couple trying to enter the U.S. as a married couple the "latest pair of domestic terrorists."

That is what marriage would do for us. It would provide us with more than 1,138 rights and legitimize our relationships. Now that's liberation!

fourteen

Lefties Are
the Spawn of
Satan...

"I think that the people who are caught up in the homosexual lifestyle need help. We encourage people to stop smoking. This federal marriage resolution is the same sort of thing." —Tom McMillin, Oakland County, Mich., Commissioner

The Bible contains more than 100 favorable references to the right hand and 25 unfavorable references to the left hand.

Today, no one would take seriously a person who went around spouting that "Left-handed people are the spawn of Satan!" It's absurd! Yet in times past, because left-handed people were statistically less significant, ignorant people created misguided beliefs that left-handers must be the product of something evil, much as ignorant people still hold on to a belief that gays and lesbians are sinners.

Gays and lesbians are statistically less significant than heterosexuals, but does this mean the law should discriminate against us? I understand that there will always be stares and lots of questions from well-meaning or uninformed people who have never seen a same-sex parented family, but people with disabilities and interracial couples have to deal with that too. Certainly more people would be up in arms if, say, redheads, albinos, and left-handers were denied the right to marry altogether—or if they were forced to marry only non-redheads, non-albinos, and right-handers—instead of being given the choice like everyone else, the choice to marry whomever they love.

Just because we are only 10% of the population doesn't mean that we should feel comfortable with less than 100% of our national rights and protections.

> *"Most Americans do not want persons who openly engage in homosexual conduct as partners in their business, as scoutmasters for their children, as teachers in their children's schools, or as boarders in their home."*
> —Justice Antonin Scalia in dissent of *Lawrence v. Texas,* issued June 26, 2003

It really wasn't so long ago that left-handers were forced to use their right hands and punished when they deviated, much the same way that LGBT people have been subjected to shock therapy, curative self-help groups, and talk therapy, and advised to pray harder and attend church more frequently to rid themselves of the disease—or the evil—of homosexuality. But nowadays we have come to accept left-handed people as nothing more than left-handed people. Sure, some folks may still remark, "Oh, you're a leftie." But past brief curiosity, it's not an issue. That's why we don't need "left-handed pride" parades. Left-handers can easily be out of the closet and are no longer forced to awkwardly use their right hands. I hope the same thing will someday be true for LGBT people.

Stanley Kurtz, conservative marriage equality opponent and research fellow at Stanford University, says in his plea against same-sex marriage that "the right to marry would symbolize social approval for homosexuality" ("Beyond Gay Marriage," *The Weekly Standard*, Aug 4/11, 2003). Would he have presented a similar argument a few decades earlier when the majority of whites were against interracial marriage? What's wrong with social approval for gay people anyway? Sure, we're statistically less significant, but we're not insane or socially deviant as we were once made out to be. Hatemongers perpetuate the belief that we are morally inferior individuals who choose to partake in a "vice," and that we are therefore unworthy of the institution of marriage. But you don't see religious zealots clamoring to take marriage rights away from adulterers, gamblers, smokers, alcoholics, criminals, or even convicted child molesters.

Some may chuckle and find it hard to believe that left-handers were persecuted and seen as willful for not using their right hands. Some may feel indignant that blacks were seen as sub-human livestock for whites to own. Others may still hold on to these beliefs—but clearly they are in the minority.

Beliefs may change over time, but the tactics used to discriminate against a minority group rarely do. Whose side are you on? The side that will one day be apologizing (like those who supported segregation) or the side that believes all people have certain inalienable rights?

"What you're doing is undermining the whole legal definition, the underpinnings of the institution of the family, and when that goes, everything goes with it, including the stability of the country and the future of Western civilization."
—Focus on the Family executive director James Dobson

Have you ever seen the crazy religious extremists who drive around in the RV with pictures of the Twin Towers on fire and Tinky Winky pointing and laughing? You know, the ones with the rainbow-colored bumper stickers that say HOMOSEXUALITY IS A SIN! Jerry Falwell and Pat Robertson's commentary on September 11, blaming gays for the terrorist attacks on the World Trade Center spurred on a whole new trend in car detailing. What's next? Vans stencil-decorated with a pair of grooms exiting the church to walk through the open gates of hell?

Believe me, there are real people out there—many of them registered voters—who are convinced that same-sex marriage will lead to Armageddon, and they are scared. They're more scared than the Y2K survivalists who bought several months of supplies and built bomb shelters in their backyards because they thought the earth would be destroyed by nukes on New Year's. They're more scared than folks who once believed the decline of Western Civilization would result from the end of slavery, and then later from integration and interracial marriage. They're reactionary and fundamentalist, like the Nazi fascists who called homosexuals "a blight" on German society. They're the sort of people who attend such events as Trinity Church's annual "Hell House" in Cedar Hill, Texas—a haunted house with a twist, designed to scare the kids by showing scenes of gay people dying of AIDS and girls dying from abortions. These folks are 100% committed to making life miserable for LGBT people. If you need to be reminded of how extreme these people are, visit Fred Phelps's godhatesfags.com.

The Anti-Equality Agenda

"I am dedicating my talents, time, and energies to the passage of an amendment to the U.S. Constitution that will protect the traditional family from its enemies who wish to legalize same-sex marriage and other diverse 'family' forms. My line in the sand has been drawn." —JERRY FALWELL

"It is adequate if the federal courts allow it to stand, but the federal courts are showing a continuing desire to ban traditional values from the public square and even recently legalized sodomy in the Texas case." —JERRY FALWELL, SPEAKING ON THE FEDERAL DEFENSE OF MARRIAGE ACT

"Traditional family breakdown is the single biggest social problem is America today. I believe Congress has an obligation to defend the legal status of marriage before the Supreme Court or individual state courts take away the public's ability to act." —SEN. RICK SANTORUM

"Thus, we strongly oppose any legislative and judicial attempts, both at state and federal levels, to grant same-sex unions the equivalent status and rights of marriage—by naming them

108

marriage, civil unions, or by any other means."
—FROM A STATEMENT OF THE ADMINISTRATIVE
COMMITTEE, UNITED STATES CONFERENCE OF
CATHOLIC BISHOPS, SEPTEMBER 9, 2003

*"The best legal minds in the country have come
to the conclusion that the only way we can protect ourselves from having the judiciary force
same-sex 'marriage' upon an unwilling nation is
to have a constitutional amendment that says
specifically that nothing in the U.S. Constitution
or any of the state constitutions shall be construed as requiring that marriage be anything
other than the union of a man and a woman,"*
—RICHARD LAND, PRESIDENT OF THE SOUTHERN
BAPTIST CONVENTION'S ETHICS AND RELIGIOUS
LIBERTY COMMISSION

WHAT THE RIGHT WING IS UP TO NOW!

Like it or not, conservative Christians have focused
their nearly exclusive attention on preventing "homosexual marriage." But the intent is more malicious than simply
defending marriage as being for heterosexuals only. Their
goals are clearly outlined by Jerry Falwell and the U.S.
Catholic Bishops to deny any protections, benefits, and
rights to "diverse family forms" or any union other than
marriage. Clearly, this is an attack on LGBT families, but
cohabiting heterosexuals will also be hurt.

Their first tactical move was the creation of the Defense
of Marriage Act (DOMA). The Defense of Marriage Act
was created in 1996 in response to Alaska and Hawaii
coming close to allowing marriage for same-sex couples.
The Defense of Marriage Act (DOMA) defined marriage
as "a legal union between one man and one woman as

husband and wife." President Clinton, the perfect poster child for the sanctity of marriage, signed the bill into law in 1996. As if that wasn't enough of an assault on equal rights, 38 states have since passed mini-DOMAs so that if same-sex marriage is ever legalized in another state, their state does not have to recognize those marriages. Imagine the state or federal government acting that quickly to pass ENDA or hate crimes legislation—or to pass a budget.

Nonetheless, the constitutionality of these laws has yet to be tested. The recent Massachusetts ruling and the possibility that the New Jersey Supreme Court may rule in favor of same-sex marriage has frightened religious conservatives and other opponents of marriage equality so much that they've begun to create a new defensive strategy: a Federal Amendment to the Constitution.

"We need to do everything we can to protect and strengthen the family. The homosexual activists are going to the courts to gain recognition for homosexual marriage."
—Marilyn Musgrave, U.S. representative from Colorado and House sponsor of the Federal Marriage Amendment

Drastic measures are called for, marriage equality opponents say, because the "black plague" (commonly known as the U.S. Supreme Court) is endorsing the "homosexual agenda" by overturning sodomy laws with the *Lawrence v. Texas* decision. Therefore, the only way to exclude same-sex couples from marriage is to change the constitution so that courts cannot declare marriage discrimination unconstitutional.

On Thursday, July 12, 2001, the Alliance for Marriage

(AFM) announced their proposal for a Constitutional Amendment titled: "The Federal Marriage Amendment." Its purpose, according to the AFM, is to strengthen American families and reintegrate the role of a strong father figure. Realistically, this is a thinly veiled attempt to ban marriage equality in the U.S.

Spearheaded by Colorado representative Marilyn Musgrave, a Christian politician closely aligned with Focus on the Family, the Federal Marriage Amendment would change the constitution by denying same-sex couples any relationship benefits, rights, or protections. The amendment would add the following two sentences to our Constitution:

1. Marriage in the United States shall consist only of the union of a man and a woman.

2. Neither this Constitution or the constitution of any state, nor state or federal law, shall be construed to require that marital status or the legal incidents thereof be conferred upon unmarried couples or groups.

The amendment requires a two-thirds vote in both the House and Senate and must be ratified by 75% of the states. Thirty-eight state constitutions have already been changed to outlaw same-sex marriage, and there is reason to believe that a federal amendment could pass as well. And sponsors have greased the amendment with a "slippery slope" fear tactic: Those voting to pass the amendment will be voting against same-sex marriage *and polygamy*. If this amendment passes, it's possible that *all* domestic partnership rights, civil union rights, and any other "marriage lite" rights same-sex couples may have or want to have in the future will be invalidated and inaccessible, rolling back the clock on the gains made thus far.

Never in the history of this country has the U.S. Constitution been changed to accommodate discrimination. To the contrary, the U.S. Constitution has been changed to provide for rights that had previously been denied, such as to give women the right to vote, and to outlaw slavery. Musgrave represents a radical antigay minority who seeks to codify its religious beliefs and deny American citizens basic civil rights. If this bill passes, it will not only ban same-sex marriage, it will effectively deny gay, lesbian, bisexual, and transsexual people the most basic of relationship rights, including the right to visit a partner in the hospital, the right to be recognized as next of kin, and the right to make medical decisions for a partner.

The Right has made marriage equality the number one wedge issue of the 2004 election, and the religious right seems to be focusing the majority of their resources on the Federal Marriage Amendment to ban same-sex marriage. They declared October 12-18, 2003 "Marriage Protection Week" and got the endorsement of Pres. George W. Bush (a great strategy to distract people from the war in Iraq and the flailing budget). On October 3, 2003, Bush used his presidential power to issue an official proclamation that stated: "Marriage is a sacred institution, and its protection is essential to the continued strength of society. Marriage Protection Week provides an opportunity to focus our efforts on preserving the sanctity of marriage and on building strong and healthy marriages in America." During "Marriage Protection Week," clergy were encouraged to give sermons against "homosexual marriage," people were told to call their congressional leaders, mayors, and governors and ask them to come out against same-sex marriage. These organizations feel that marriage equality is a violation of their religious freedom and will do whatever it takes to deny LGBT people their rights.

✆ Davina Kotulski, Ph.D. ✆

Immediate Release
Office of the Press Secretary
October 3, 2003

Marriage Protection Week, 2003
By the President of the United States of America
A Proclamation

Marriage is a sacred institution, and its protection is essential to the continued strength of our society.

Marriage Protection Week provides an opportunity to focus our efforts on preserving the sanctity of marriage and on building strong and healthy marriages in America.

Marriage is a union between a man and a woman, and my Administration is working to support the institution of marriage by helping couples build successful marriages and be good parents.

To encourage marriage and promote the well-being of children, I have proposed a healthy marriage initiative to help couples develop the skills and knowledge to form and sustain healthy marriages. Research has shown that, on average, children raised in households headed by married parents fare better than children who grow up in other
family structures. Through education and counseling programs, faith-based, community, and government organizations promote healthy marriages and a better quality of life for children. By supporting responsible child-rearing and strong families, my

113

Administration is seeking to ensure that every child can grow up in a safe and loving home.

We are also working to make sure that the Federal Government does not penalize marriage. My tax relief package eliminated the marriage penalty. And as part of the welfare reform package I have proposed, we will do away with the rules that have made it more difficult for married couples to move out of poverty.

We must support the institution of marriage and help parents build stronger families. And we must continue our work to create a compassionate, welcoming society, where all people are treated with dignity and respect.

During Marriage Protection Week, I call on all Americans to join me in expressing support for the institution of marriage with all its benefits to our people, our culture, and our society.

NOW, THEREFORE, I, GEORGE W. BUSH, President of the United States of America, by virtue of the authority vested in me by the Constitution and laws of the United States, do hereby proclaim the week of October 12 through October 18, 2003, as Marriage Protection Week. I call upon the people of the United States to observe this week with appropriate programs, activities, and ceremonies.

IN WITNESS WHEREOF, I have hereunto set my hand this third day of October, in the year of our Lord two thousand three, and of the Independence of the United

States of America the two hundred and twenty-eighth.

GEORGE W. BUSH

As Sylvia Rhue, Coalition Manager of the California Freedom to Marry, reminds, "The sacred texts of the United States are the Bill of Rights and the Declaration of Independence, and the law of this country is the U.S. Constitution, not the Bible." Yet many right-wing politicians feel compelled to force their religious beliefs on others, through faith-based government programs, prayer in school, religious monuments in the courtroom, and now by attempting to rewrite the U.S. Constitution to include blatant discrimination.

WHAT THE RIGHT WING IS UP TO NOW!

"Requiring citizens to sanction or subsidize homosexual relationships violates the freedom of conscience of millions of Christians, Jews, Muslims, and other people who believe marriage is the union of the two sexes. Civil marriage is a public act. Homosexuals are free to have a "union" ceremony with each other privately, but they are not free to demand that such a relationship be solemnized and subsidized under the law."
—Robert H. Knight, director of the Culture & Family Institute, an affiliate of Concerned Women for America. Mr. Knight was a draftsman of the federal Defense of Marriage Act of 1996.

Despite Ms. Musgrave's failure to separate church and state and Bob Knight's belief that one group of people's "freedom of conscience" is more important than another group of people's civil liberties, many religious communities already support the civil rights of same-sex couples. However, no religious denomination—regardless of its stance on blessings of same-sex couples—has the legal standing to confer those rights to same-sex couples because civil marriage is a contractual arrangement with federal and state governments.

Our neighbors to the north have realized that denying same-sex couples the right to marry is unconstitutional, as did the high courts in Vermont, Hawaii, and Massachusetts. We must protect the U.S. Constitution against its enemies and fight against the Federal Marriage Amendment.

If you still think it's not really that bad, check out the Alliance Defense Fund's Web site at www.alliancedefensefund.org. Go to the "homosexual agenda" button entitled "How to Receive Your Copy of The Homosexual Agenda: Exposing the Principal Threat to Religious Freedom." The Web site states that your contribution of "$35 or more to help the Alliance Defense Fund win the legal battle for religious freedom, family values, and the sanctity of human life." The ADF actually funds training seminars for attorneys and internships for law students on how to defeat gay issues. They even meet quarterly to discuss what "gay issues" they are going to take on next. The ADF's Web site has links to disturbing articles about the organization's agenda of continuing to defeat all rights for gay people. One article has the surreal title: "Pray for Canada, Pray for us."

These organizations are not few and far between. As noted in an October 17, 2003 report by the National Gay and Lesbian Task Force ("Marriage Protection Week Sponsors: are they really interested in building strong and healthy marriages?"), these entities are organized and viciously antigay. They are also fiscally powerful, wielding a combined annual budget of $217 million per year compared to $54 million budget of the top LGBT rights group. The NGLTF report found that of the 29 organizations involved in "Marriage Protection Week," one organization (Focus on the Family) alone had an annul budget $126 million. In addition, the Ethics and Religious Liberty

Commission, the official ministry of the public policy arm of the Southern Baptist Convention, is America's second largest religious denomination. The report concluded that organizational cosponsors of Marriage Protection Week focus excessively on homosexuality over key issues that impact marriage and families, such as divorce, lack of health insurance, domestic violence, and poverty. The report also noted that these organizations "capitalize and profit from homophobia in order to fund their broader political agendas," including denial of a woman's right to choose to have an abortion and "no-fault" divorce.

To assess how concerned these organizations were about real threats to families NGLTF scoured the Marriage Protection Week cosponsor's Web sites for documents on homosexuality in comparison to domestic violence, health insurance, and other issues. The findings were sobering:

> The American Family Association had 334 documents containing the word "homosexual," only 47 with the word "divorce," 29 with the word "poverty," 17 with the words "domestic violence," 5 with the words "child support," and 4 with "health insurance."
>
> Concerned Women for America had 602 documents on its Web site that contain the word "homosexual," but only 80 with "poverty," only 70 with the word "divorce," 19 with the words "domestic violence" and only 6 containing "child support."

In conclusion, NGLTF found that on the Web sites of "Marriage Protection Week" cosponsors there were 2,369 documents on homosexuality, compared with 1,432 on divorce, 834 on poverty, 207 for health insurance, 190 on domestic violence, and 85 on child support. Clearly, "Marriage Protection Week" cosponsors have a skewed notion about threats to the average family's stability. They feel entitled to use blatant discrimination to justify their acts of prejudice and rally calls for psychological and physical violence against LGBT people through their use of antigay religious rhetoric and biblical passages.

"We are not tolerant of behaviors that destroy individuals, families, and our culture. Individuals may be free to pursue such behaviors as sodomy, but we will not and cannot tolerate these behaviors...In short, we believe in intolerance to those things that are evil; and we believe that we should discriminate against those behaviors which are dangerous to individuals and society."
—Lou Sheldon, Traditional Values Coalition

fifteen

Marriage Rights
in the U.S.
and Around the Globe

BOSTON MARRIAGES?

July 2003 was a time when everyone was waiting on pins and needles for the Massachusetts Supreme Court to make a decision. LGBT people and fair-minded citizens hoped that the United States would follow in the footsteps of its neighbor Canada and change history. Christian conservatives, on the other hand, were panicking and trying to figure out how to stop this decision. Since the decriminalization of sodomy, some touched-in-the-head folks were even calling for a united prayer effort—for U.S. Supreme Court justices to drop dead! Who knew what Pandora's box would be opened next? But July passed without a word from the bench, then August, September, October, still nothing.

Then, on November 18, the court seemed to be approaching a breakthrough. Marriage activists from around the country started down their phone-tree lists, while scouts surveyed the Gay & Lesbian Advocates and Defenders (GLAD) Web page, and channel-surfed between MSNBC and CNN.

Finally, the headlines rang out.

MASSACHUSETTS COURT STRIKES DOWN BAN ON
SAME-SEX MARRIAGE

MASS. HIGH COURT OK'S GAY MARRIAGE

Spontaneous support rallies erupted, and people around the country celebrated an early Thanksgiving with Boston baked beans, cranberry juice, and Boston cream pies. But the celebration may have jumped the gun: At the time of this writing, no state has issued a same-sex couple a marriage license.

The Massachusetts Supreme Judicial Court stated clearly that the state's constitution "affirms the dignity and equality of all individuals" and "forbids the creation of second-class citizens," but they still fell short of immediately issuing the plaintiff couples marriage licenses. Instead the court issued a 180-day stay "to permit the legislature to take such action as it may deem appropriate in light of this opinion."

On Feb. 4, 2004, following a request from the Massachusetts legislature to clarify whether enacting civil unions or some other legal equivalent would satisfy the intent of the opinion, the court confirmed that nothing less than full marriage equality was sufficient to pass the muster under the state constitution's equal protection guarantee.

Anti-equality Massachusetts governor Mitt Romney and Massachusetts attorney general Thomas F. Riledy say they intend to convene a state constitutional convention to define marriage so as to exlude same-sex couples. However, the process requires that the proposed amendment be ratified in two consecutive legislative sessions, then approved by a majority vote on a ballot measure. The soonest such a change could be effective under this process is November, 2005, after same-sex couples will have been legally marrying for more than two years.

Massachusetts, Here We Come?

While it's not clear how Massachusetts will play out, what is clear is that marriage in Massachusetts will not solve our problems in the immediate future. The 38 states with mini-DOMA's do not have to recognize marriages that are not "between a man and a woman," nor does the federal government. Same-sex couples in Vermont civil unions would have to dissolve their civil unions to get married. For nonresident couples in Vermont civil unions, at least one partner would have to live in Vermont for six months before the union could be dissolved to allow the couple to apply for a Massachusetts marriage license.

Also, because a number of states—including California—have laws banning marriage between same-sex couples, applying for a Massachusetts marriage license may threaten a couple's domestic partnership status.

In the Meantime...

Prepare for a backlash and start working to educate everyone around you about the importance of full marriage equality at the federal and state level. If you go to Massachusetts for a marriage license, be prepared to have it seen as merely symbolic once you leave Massachusetts. Legal experts at GLAD, Lambda Legal, NCLR, and Freedom to Marry all agree that same-sex couples should carefully consider choosing whether to litigate in order to have their marriages legitimized. According to GLAD, "it is critical to

A case that turns out badly can create a bad law.

remember that any legal case has profound implications beyond the individuals involved." It's important that couples don't pursue marriage litigation in their states without first consulting one of the above-mentioned legal groups and without a solid grass-roots educational campaign in place.

We must work together as marriage activists and educators, not marriage mavericks. This is especially true for cases that are challenging a federal statute. If you have been discriminated against and want to challenge that discrimination, contact Gay & Lesbian Advocates and Defenders (GLAD), the National Center for Lesbian Rights (NCLR), Lambda Legal, and Freedom to Marry and explain your situation. Contact information for these organizations can be found on pages 184–188.

HAWAII RECIPROCAL BENEFICIARIES

According to Courtney Joslin, J.D., attorney at the National Center for Lesbian Rights, "In 1993, the Hawaii State Supreme Court was the first court to rule that denying same-sex couples the freedom to marry could violate the state constitution because it discriminated on the basis of sex." Joslin noted that the court also found that arguments used to deny interracial marriages before the 1960s were "strikingly similar" to those used to deny same-sex couples the right to marry. God's will was used to justify discrimination in both cases. A Virginia Judge supporting the ban against interracial marriages in 1967 stated:

Almighty God created the races white, black, yellow, Malay, and red, and he placed them on separate continents. And but for the interference with his arrangement, there would be no such cause for such marriages. The fact that he separated the races shows that he did not intend for the races to mix.

Fortunately, the Supreme Court saw through that argument, and ruled in favor of allowing interracial couples the right to marry. In 1998 Hawaii courts also turned a deaf ear to this bogus interpretation of "God's will" and ruled that "constitutional law may mandate, like it or not, that customs change with an evolving social order."

While it looked like Hawaii would be the first state to legalize same-sex marriage, a ballot initiative passed by Hawaii's voters in 1998 changed the state's constitution to state that a civil marriage could only be between a man and a woman. (Opponents of equality are scurrying to prepare a similar measure in Massachusetts.)

Even though Hawaiian same-sex couples were ultimately denied marriage rights, the state did provide a compromise by creating a new beast: the reciprocal beneficiary. According to Joslin, this law provides that any two unmarried people, as long as they may not be married under Hawaii marriage law (such as same-sex couples or immediate family members), may confer health care and other rights onto each other. Additional rights include inheritance rights, survivorship benefits, health-related rights such as hospital visitation, family and funeral leave, private and public employee prepaid health insurance coverage, motor vehicle insurance coverage, jointly held property rights such as tenancy in the entirety and public land leases, legal standing for wrongful death and crime victims rights, and other benefits related to the use of state facilities and state properties.

VERMONT CIVIL UNIONS

In December of 1999 the Vermont Supreme Court ruled that denying same-sex couples the benefits and protections of civil marriage was a violation of the state's constitution. Vermont chose to create a separate institution: civil unions. Vermont's civil union law went into effect in July 2000. It gives same-sex couples all the state-conferred rights and protections available to heterosexuals in the state of Vermont, except—of course—the emotional benefits and recognition that come with the word *marriage*. Civil unions are not recognized outside Vermont, and persons united in a civil union do not have access to the 1,138 federal rights that accompany civil marriage.

California Domestic Partnerships

Openly lesbian assembly member Carol Midgen introduced, and California governor Gray Davis signed into law, the first statewide domestic partnership registry in 1999, effective in January 2000. At first the registry offered only one right: to visit a sick partner in the hospital as next of kin. In October 2001 another 13 rights were added to the registry, and the right to inherit without a will was added in 2002. On Sept. 19, 2003, Davis signed AB 205, the California Domestic Partner Rights and Responsibilities Act, which grants California registered domestic partners almost all of the state rights associated with civil marriage. At the time of this writing, it appears that AB 205 will go into effect as planned on Jan. 1, 2005.

The 38 Anti-Equality States
and the Undeclared

Thirty-eight states have mini-DOMAs. Those without mini-DOMAs are Connecticut, Maryland, Massachusetts, New Hampshire, New Jersey, New Mexico, New York, Oregon, Rhode Island, Vermont, Wisconsin, Wyoming, and the District of Columbia. Many of these states have pending same-sex marriage lawsuits—as well as pending right-to-marry legislation—but they are also being targeted with anti-equality measures. They are true battlegrounds.

MARRIAGE CASES PENDING

"Marriage is one of the basic civil rights of man, fundamental to our very existence and survival."
—U.S. Supreme Court, *Loving v. Virginia*, 1967

New Jersey currently has a marriage case pending, but the case is still in its infancy. Other cases may emerge in the other 13 states where no DOMA yet exists.

Several lawsuits to legalize same-sex marriage have gone poorly. First, there was the marriage case in Alaska, then the ACLU's case in Indiana was shot down. More recently, a court in Arizona ruled against a same-sex couple who had argued that since sodomy was legal they should be able to legally marry. The court concluded: "The fundamental right to marry protected by our federal and state constitutions does not encompass the right to marry a same-sex partner. Moreover, although many traditional views of homosexuality have been recast over time on our state and nation, the choice to marry a same-sex partner has not taken sufficient root to receive constitutional protection as a fundamental right." The court argued that it was "for the people of Arizona, through their elected representatives or by using the initiative process, rather than the court, to decide whether to permit same-sex marriage."

If judges who are supposed to be fair don't do their jobs without bigotry why would a majority of Arizona voters? In this context it's unsettling to recall that in 1968 *The New York Times* published a Gallup poll revealing that only 20% of Americans approved of marriages between whites and nonwhites—a full year after the Supreme Court had declared bans on interracial marriages as unconstitutional.

126

PRO- AND ANTI-EQUALITY LEGISLATION

"When I was married approximately 44 years ago, it was illegal in 30-something states in this nation because my wife happened to be white. I knew if I went into Virginia, I could be arrested, but it didn't stop me from marrying. There may be states that do crazy things, but when we're finished, we'll end up being the law of the land." —Herman "Denny" Farrell Jr., New York State Assembly member and state Democratic committee chairman referring to the Right to Marry bill

The "Right to Marry" bill has been introduced into the New York State Senate by Tom Duane and in the Assembly by Dick Gottfried. Other supportive Democrats attached to this bill are: Sen. Liz Krueger, Assembly Member Scott Stringer, and Assembly Member Jonathan Bing. However, under Republican Senate Majority Leader Joseph Bruno, who opposes same-sex marriage, the bill does not have much of a chance of being heard.

Legislation to legalize same-sex marriage has also been introduced in Rhode Island, Hawaii, Maryland, Wisconsin, Vermont, and most recently in California. Anti-equality measures are pending in New York, as well as in Massachusetts, New Jersey, and Wisconsin. Visit www.marriageequalityny.org for up-to-date information on gay marriage battles throughout the country.

BEYOND U.S. BORDERS

Three countries currently offer marriage licenses to same-sex couples: the Netherlands, Canada, and Belgium. The Netherlands was the first country to do so on Apr. 1, 2001. In January 2003 Belgium followed suit, and in June

2003 two Canadian provinces (Ontario and British Columbia) did as well. These marriages are not recognized in other countries.

THE NETHERLANDS

Since Apr. 1, 2003, the Netherlands has provided same-sex couples the benefits and responsibilities of marriage. However, there are restrictions. Residency requirements dictate that one member of the couple must be a citizen of the Netherlands or reside there. The Netherlands does allow adoption by same-sex couples. The adoption law was changed at the same time the marriage law changed in 2001. A woman can now legally adopt her wife's biological child. Also, gay couples can adopt Dutch children. What they can't do is adopt foreign children as a couple. But many people have found a way around this. One partner can adopt abroad, and after a few years the other partner can adopt the child in the Netherlands. Married Dutch gay men are now adopting in the U.S. and South Africa as a single parent because these countries allow single gay people to adopt.

BELGIUM

Much like the Netherlands, Belgium has some restrictions that pose serious problems for LGBT families. First, only Belgian citizens or people who live in other countries that allow same-sex marriage can marry. Second, like the Netherlands, Belgium denies same-sex couples the right to adopt children. Interestingly, in the United States, LGBT people can adopt children, but they can't have marriage rights. Go figure!

CANADA

As of June 2003, two Canadian provinces, Ontario and British Columbia, allow same-sex couples the right to marry. In 2002 the Quebec high court ruled that same-sex marriage discrimination cannot be justified under the Charter of Rights and Freedoms but suspended its declaration for two years in order to give Parliament time to act on the matter. The governments of several provinces as well as the Law Commission of Canada, the Canadian Human Rights Commission, and an array of groups have called for an end to same-sex marriage discrimination nationwide.

A decision on a national law for full marriage equality in Canada is expected some time in 2004. On October 30, 2003, the attorney general of Canada issued a factum to the Supreme Court of Canada containing arguments in support of proposed legislation that would extend full marriage equality across the country. The court will hear all arguments, on both sides, beginning in April 2004.

For the time being, same-sex couples who are legally married in Ontario and British Columbia enjoy all the rights given to heterosexual married couples in those provinces. Until a national law is enacted or another province gives the green light to marriage equality, same-sex marriages are not recognized outside British Columbia or Ontario.

Unlike the Netherlands and Belgium, Canada has no residency requirements. Adoption became legal for gay couples in Ontario in 1998, five years prior to legalization of same-sex marriage in this province.

Marriage Canadian-Style

American same-sex partners who get married in Canada face a host of uncertainties. According to Shannon Minter, legal director for the National Center for Lesbian Rights, getting married in Canada may have serious tax and legal implications.

Same-sex couples need to consider the pros and cons of getting married in Canada very seriously. According to

Minter, once you obtain a marriage license, locate an authorized person to perform the ceremony, and arrange for two witnesses to be present during the ceremony, you will still return to a country that refuses to recognize your marriage. "Some state and local governments will acknowledge your marriage, at least for some purposes. Others will not," Minter says. "The same is true for private employers and businesses." As long as the federal DOMA is still in place, "the federal government will almost certainly refuse to respect your marriage," he adds.

But because the marriage is valid, whether it's recognized as such or not, dissolution is a serious topic to contend with. Minter advises that to obtain a divorce at least one partner must live in Canada for a minimum of one year before a Canadian court will have jurisdiction to grant one. Those who have already taken the Canadian plunge better hope love will keep them together.

Another complication arises when it comes to taxes. Even seasoned LGBT legal advisers in the States cannot say for sure if same-sex couples married in Canada will be able to file joint federal and state income taxes—and what will happen to them if they do or don't. But it does appear that same-sex couples married in Canada or united in Vermont civil unions are more likely to be audited by the IRS. According to Minter, these couples are caught in a double bind: Current federal law prohibits the validity of same-sex marriage, yet *all* married couples are legally required to pay taxes as married couples.

The federal DOMA must be overturned and same-sex marriage legalized in the United States. If not, couples married in Canada will be in the same situation as interracial couples in the 1960s and before, legally married in some countries and states, and legal strangers or lawbreakers in others. Remember that 1968 Gallup poll in which only 20% of Americans approved of marriages between whites and nonwhites? That was the lowest percentage of approval among the 13 countries surveyed. The second lowest country, at 29%, was Great Britain, Uruguay 30%, Norway 35%, West Germany 35%, Canada 36%, Austria 39%, Switzerland 50%, Greece 50%, Netherlands 51%, Finland 58%, France 62%, and Sweden 67%. Swayed by reactionary movements, the United States lags behind other Westernized countries when it comes to social progress.

"The human rights of homosexuals have been gradually recognized by countries around the world. To protect their rights, people should have the right to wed and have a family based on their free will."
—Taiwan presidential office, as reported in the United Daily News, October 2003

The idea of civil unions and same-sex marriage is not a new concept. Denmark has had registered partnerships since 1989. Norway (1993), Greenland (1994), Sweden (1995), and Iceland (1996) have also recognized some form of domestic partnerships or civil unions for close to a decade. France began recognizing the partnerships of same-sex couples in 1999, and Germany followed suit shortly thereafter. Other countries that provide some recognition of same-sex couples' rights include Australia, Brazil, Finland, Portugal, Hungary, Israel, and Italy.

Same-sex marriage is now being hotly debated throughout the world. According to Marriage Equality USA, Nobel Peace Prize winner Archbishop Desmond Tutu of South Africa has called discrimination against lesbian and gay men "the moral equivalent of apartheid," and declared lesbian and gay equality as "the world's next moral goal." Many countries are considering the legalization of same-sex marriage or civil unions, including South Africa, the United Kingdom, New Zealand, the Czech Republic, Finland, Luxembourg, Portugal, Spain, and Switzerland; parts of Asia want in on the action too. According to the *United Daily News*, in October 2003 the presidential office of Taiwan and the cabinet plan to legalize gay marriage and recognize the right of same-sex couples to adopt children.

In Spain three couples, including a Madrid city council member, are challenging same-sex marriage inequality. Lawsuits have been filed in Madrid and Valencia. The Basque provinces, Andalusia, Catalonia, and Navarra already provide some protections, such as adoption rights, spousal health care coverage, and joint income-tax filing status to both gay and unmarried straight couples.

A November 2003 poll conducted by the British government found that "eight out of 10 Britons support legislation recognizing same-sex domestic partnerships." On November 26, 2003, the Queen made a speech to Parliament that unveiled the Civil Partnership Bill. The bill covers same-sex couples in England and Wales. While the bill would not grant full marriage status, it would provide many benefits enjoyed by married heterosexual couples, such as allowing a surviving partner to receive pension benefits, recognition of a partner as next of kin when dealing with hospitals, and exempting a surviving partner from paying inheritance tax on the deceased's home.

sixteen

Parenting

"According to an Urban Institute analysis, commissioned by the HRC Foundation, compared with opposite-sex couples, same-sex couples are having children at about the same rate as opposite sex couples in many states, including California, Illinois, New Jersey, New York, Ohio, Texas, and Massachusetts." —from an HRC report, June 27, 2003

A Tale of Two Sperms

Jane and John, a married heterosexual couple, go to the sperm bank because they want to have a child and John is infertile. They pick out a nice donor and after several withdrawals and deposits, *voilà*, Jane is pregnant.

And now...the same scenario, only the sexes are changed!

Jane and Jan, a same-sex couple, go to the sperm bank because they also want to have a child. After several attempts, Jane becomes pregnant.

To the naked eye of common sense, it looks like all things are equal: one biological parent, one nonbiological parent, and one anonymous donor. And really, all things *should* be equal—but they aren't! It doesn't matter whose sperm it is. When it comes down to legal rights, civil marriage matters most.

Because of their civil marriage, when Jane and John have their child, each of their names automatically goes down on the child's birth certificate. But for Jane and Jan, the ordeal is just beginning. After the baby is born, only Jane (the biological parent) appears on the child's birth certificate. The nonbiological parent, Jan, is still considered a legal stranger, unless her state allows her to go through either a second-parent adoption or a stepparent adoption.

SECOND-PARENT ADOPTIONS

According to the National Center for Lesbian Rights (NCLR)—which created the concept of second-parent adoption in the early 1980's—a second-parent adoption (or co-parent adoption) is a legal procedure allowing a same-sex parent to adopt her or his partner's biological or adoptive child without terminating the first parent's legal status as a parent. Second-parent adoptions protect children in same-sex parent families by giving them the security of two legal parents.

But second-parent adoption also protects the rights of the second parent by making sure that he or she will continue to have a legally recognized parental relationship to the child in case the couple separates, or if the biological (or original adoptive parent) dies or becomes incapacitated.

Since its inception the procedure has been established in California and several other states. Second-parent adoptions can be attained by statute or appellate court decision in 10 states (California, Connecticut, the District of Columbia, Illinois, Indiana, Massachusetts, Pennsylvania, New York, New Jersey, and Vermont), and in specific areas in at least 15 others: Alabama (selected counties), Alaska (Juneau), Delaware (selected counties), Hawaii (selected counties), Indiana (White County), Iowa (selected counties), Louisiana (Orleans Parish), Maryland (selected counties), Minnesota (Aitkin and Hennepin Counties), Nevada (selected counties), New Mexico (selected counties), Oregon (Multnomah County), Rhode Island (selected counties), Texas (Austin, San Antonio, and other selected counties), Washington (King, Spokane, Thurston, and other selected counties).

Second-parent adoptions have been denied in Colorado, Nebraska, Ohio, and Wisconsin. Arkansas, Mississippi, Utah, and Florida do not allow gays or lesbians to adopt children, period.

STEPPARENT ADOPTIONS

One of the provisions of AB 25, which California governor Gray Davis signed on October 14, 2001, allows lesbians and gay men who are registered domestic partners access to a procedure previously reserved for heterosexual married couples. Now same-sex domestic partners can become stepparents to each other's biological or adopted children.

A November 2001 article published by the National Center for Lesbian Rights, titled "The Transition From Second-Parent Adoptions to Stepparent Adoptions After AB 25," outlines how this procedure works:

> The partner who is not already a legal parent files a petition for adoption. This is the same form as used for second-parent adoptions, but different boxes are checked.
>
> The adoption petition is forwarded to the county agency or independent social worker responsible for investigating stepparent adoptions in the county in which the couple resides.

The social worker completes an investigation, usually consisting of a meeting with both parents, completion of a questionnaire, receipt of several positive references from friends of the couple, and a medical and background check on the adopting parent. The investigation generally takes from three to six months. The social worker also obtains the formal consent of the legal parent and of any parent giving up parental rights to allow the adoption to be completed.

The social worker writes a report, which s/he forwards to the court. The couple then goes to court for a brief hearing, at which the adoption is granted. Following the granting of the adoption, a new birth certificate is issued by Sacramento (assuming the child was born in California), listing the legal parent and the adopting parent as the child's parents.

Despite advances in legal protections offered to same-sex couples, second-parent and stepparent adoptions continue to be lengthy, costly, and intrusive. Moreover, they unfairly target same-sex parents, and involve at least one home visit from a social worker.

Depending on their state of residence, Jane and Jan may end up paying around $4,000; then they may have to wait about a year, arrange for a home study and home visit, and apply to the courts. If all goes well, then and only then, will each woman be considered her child's legal parent. There is no surefire way to circumvent this rigmarole—even if one of the women was to donate an egg, have it fertilized, and then have it inserted into her partner's uterus!

THE BITTER FRUIT OF DISCRIMINATION:
EMOTIONAL, LEGAL, AND FINANCIAL REPERCUSSIONS

"Because we weren't married, we were worried that people were going to take our child away from us. Without marriage our families didn't have the opportunity to go through the process of becoming one family. We had to do that through legal documentation that was awkward. The legal process I went through was to become a second-parent to my child which is something stepparents do. It was kind of like becoming a parent through the backdoor, all that just to be recognized as my son's mother." —April Fernando

The legal process of securing parental rights for a non-biological same-sex parent is excruciatingly painful for the family and can create a tentative quality to the parent-child relationship. Child psychologist and nonbiological mother April Fernando notes, "It's been a real education and until I had the paper that said that I was my son's parent, there was something a little touch-and-go about our relationship, because the legal aspects of being a parent are so important, even though we may not know them all on a conscious level." Dr. Fernando and her partner, Jen, took a number of legal steps, including drafting wills, powers of attorney, and a legal decree stating that Dr. Fernando would be able to make medical decisions for their unborn child if anything happened to Jen. Despite all these precautions, the entire adoption process made the couple feel "less than." Also, the adoption process can often be a brutal reminder of the suspiciousness people harbor toward LGBT parents raising children. "Going through the process of adoption, they evaluate whether or not you are 'fit to be a parent,' " Dr. Fernando says. "I think everyone should go through it, not just me because I'm gay."

THAT AIN'T MY KID!

A child born to two parents in a heterosexual marriage, whether through alternative insemination or surrogacy, is the legal responsibility of both parents. A child born through a surrogate or alternative insemination to two mothers or two fathers is at risk for emotional and financial abandonment by the nonbiological parent.

In *Bendz v. El Dorado Superior Court*, the nonbiological parent of two children, Ry and Kaia, separated from their biological mother and refused to pay child support. The nonbio mother asserted that Ry and Kaia were not her kids. This case is particularly cruel in that the nonbiological mother turned her back on a special needs child; she fled from her responsibilities as a parent, leaving her ex to handle it all alone. Luckily, in 2003 the trial court ruled that under the California Uniform Parentage Act "by virtue of consenting to the insemination with the intention of parenting the resulting children," the nonbiological mother was responsible for them. However, this ruling is currently on appeal.

CUSTODY ISSUES

There continue to be numerous cases in which a nonbiological parent is denied access to his or her own children and considered a legal stranger by the courts. Many of these cases occur with the dissolution of the relationship, others with the death of the biological parent.

If you watch *Court TV*, the name Michael Kantaras probably rings a bell. *Kantaras v. Kantaras* was the 21st Century version of *Kramer v. Kramer*. Michael Kantaras's wife challenged her ex-husband's right to custody by calling the marriage "a sham" because Michael was a female-to-male (FTM) transsexual. (Michael had transitioned from female to male two years before their marriage.) In a televised court proceeding viewed round the country, Michael's parents verified that Michael had always been a man trapped in a woman's body, had pitched fits when forced to wear a dress, and was in their eyes their son. Kantaras's ex, on the other hand, took advantage of mean-spirited homophobic laws and urged the court to rule that their marriage was null and void. The courts ruled in favor of Michael Kantaras, affirming his marriage as valid because it constituted a "heterosexual marriage."

Linda Kantaras was not the only nasty mommy who decided to use homophobic laws to gain full custody. Sharon S. (referred to in a previous chapter as "Bad Sharon") used the lack of marriage protections to challenge second-parent adoptions in California. Although the trial court rejected her arguments, Sharon S. appealed to the California Court of Appeals, which ruled in her favor. Sharon's ex-partner appealed to the California Supreme Court, which overturned the previous ruling and confirmed that second-parent adoptions are valid in California.

But according to a recent summary by Lambda Legal, there are still many cases pending in which a biological parent uses the lack of legal protections as a means to justify denying child visitation rights to the nonbiological parent. In *Kristine H. v. Lisa R.*, biological mother Kristine refused to let her ex, Lisa, have visitation rights and sought to nullify a judicial declaration stating that both she and Lisa would be their daughter's legal parents. Prior to their breakup, Kristine and Lisa had been together for 10 years and had co-parented their daughter for two years.

The biological parent's death can threaten the stability of a family, leaving a legal void into which mean-spirited relatives can swoop down to remove children from the nonbiological parent. Because same-sex couples don't have the protections of civil marriage, the courts or other relatives can easily dissolve a family unit.

One such case, litigated in California with the help of Lambda Legal, concerned the guardianship of Lydia M. Ramos, who was born to Lydia S. Ramos (nonbiological parent) and Linda Rodriguez-Ramos (biological parent). When Lydia M. was 11, Linda was killed in a car accident. On the day of Linda's funeral, Linda's relatives took the child away from Lydia S. Moreover, they disallowed telephone contact with the child and refused to reveal where she was being kept. Despite Linda and Lydia's church wedding, Linda's relatives did not recognize Lydia as the child's parent. Because the state did not recognize their wedding as legal, Lydia was separated from her daughter and had to pursue litigation to get her back. Eventually, Lambda attorneys were able to "unite mother and daughter and to secure full custody of Little Lydia for Lydia," but it is unconscionable that the two had to endure this traumatic experience.

In *McKee v. Fritz* in California, a mother and father who had not spoken to their daughter in 14 years attempted to take custody of their grandchild, a teenage girl they had never even met. Stephanie and Luci had been together for 18 years when Luci died of cancer. (They had raised two children together—one borne by each woman.) When Luci died, the McKees sought to remove teenaged Christine from Stephanie Fritz's care and to separate her from her sister, Heather. According to NCLR, "After a year of litigation, a trial court dismissed all of the grandparents' claims and ordered them to pay Stephanie's attorneys fees."

However, just when Stephanie and her children thought they could put the whole ordeal behind them, the Social Security Administration refused to provide child survivor benefits to Heather, Luci's nonbiological daughter. The National Center for Lesbian Rights got involved in the case and, after an expensive and extensive appeal process, was able to get the Social Security Administration to agree that Heather was entitled to the same benefits as her sister. "Had Stephanie and Luci been able to marry, the family would not have been forced to endure this terrible litigation in their period of mourning the loss of their mother and life partner," notes NCLR.

Kids Say the Darndest Things...

"Daddy, why can't we live near Grandma in Florida?"
"Because, sweetie, your Poppa and I would be considered legal strangers in those states. We've got to stay in Vermont for the rest of our lives, or we won't be considered a family anymore."
"But don't you love Poppa?"
"Of course—I love him very much."
"But my teacher said that when two people love each other they get married..."

"IF YOU LOVE HIM SO MUCH, WHY DON'T YOU MARRY HIM?"

These words are similar to the ones spoken by the daughter of one of the Massachusetts marriage case plaintiffs. Apparently, the little girl felt uncertain about her parents' commitment to each other because they were not married. She feared that her family was going to split up or that her parents didn't really love each other as much as, say, Timmy and Amy's parents did.

The couple had to explain to their 8-year-old daughter that they were unmarried, not because they didn't love each other, but because the law, the government, and the majority of straight people felt that they didn't deserve to have the same rights as other families and that they should be happy settling for lesser things like domestic partnerships and civil unions.

In a conversation Julie Goodridge, plaintiff in the Massachusetts Goodridge decision, had with anti-gay governor Mitt Romney, she asked what she should tell her daughter if Romney passed a constitutional amendment banning same-sex marriage. "How old is she?" he reportedly asked. "Eight," Goodridge replied. "Well, what have you been telling her for the last seven years? Just keep telling her that!"

Johnny Symons, filmmaker and father of two children, stated that when his son Zachary, was two-and-a-half years old, he came home from school and exclaimed, "You GUYS can't get married!" Johnny said it sounded like Zachary was repeating what some adult told him. "Daddy and I may not be able to legally marry," he explained to his son, "but that doesn't mean we don't have a partnership and a commitment to each other."

"SHE'S NOT MY STEPMOM!"

Nothing could have been more offensive to Abby, a 17-year-old girl raised by two lesbian moms, than the day her nonbiological Mom was finally awarded legal rights to her child. Why? Because in Abby's eyes her "birthmother and non-birthmother" had been equal parents all along. They were not, however, equal in the eyes of the law. The courts deemed Abby's mom as "step-mother," not "mother," despite how Abby had referred and related to her for 17 years. What some may see as a joyous day for this family was just another painful reminder of discrimination against LGBT families.

"Are Your Parents Still Married?"

"I've never known how to answer that!" Dani, my 22-year-old hairdresser, tells me. Dani is the product of the gay baby boom. She has two moms and a gay sperm-donor dad. She tells me about how it has always hurt her when people ask if her parents are still married. "My parents were never allowed to be married in the first place!" she says emphatically, cutting dangerously close to my ear.

While Dani has no regrets about having two moms, she does have feelings about the way her moms have been treated as a couple. One way she feels her parents' second-class status affected her is that she values traditional marriage less. She is in a long-term committed relationship with a man and has two children, but Dani says she never really saw herself having a wedding or being a bride. "If my parents can't get married, then I won't either!" she says.

By refusing to enter into a marriage, Dani has denied her family access to 1,138+ legal rights and protections. Like Dani growing up, her son may not have access to his nonbiological parent's health insurance. The man who is his "stepfather" in all but the legal sense cannot claim him as a dependent when filing income taxes. He cannot legally pick Dani's son up from school, visit him in the hospital, or participate in parent-teacher conferences.

Foster Kids

And what about those children who'd give anything for a set of loving parents? What about the children Rosie O'Donnell brought into our living rooms? Many adoption agencies and foster care agencies continue to deny same-sex couples the right to adopt or foster a child, justifying their denial on—get this!—the basis that same-sex couples can not legally marry and therefore cannot provide the stability a married couple can provide. According to Lambda Legal, "Opponents of equality are using child welfare systems in Virginia, Georgia, and elsewhere to make bigoted political statements about gay people, rather than to focus on providing care for young people desperately in need."

"Sometimes when foster parents find out the child is going to be adopted by a gay couple, they will interfere and stop an adoption from going through, stating that they have changed their minds and want to adopt the child. Then after the gay couple is out of the picture, they'll change their minds again."
—Johnny Symons

It's simple: As long as gay Americans are treated as second-class citizens by family and marriage laws, all of society pays. Children in the foster care system will continue to go unplaced, moved from group home to group home, or from foster home to foster home, when they could have two loving parents.

LOVE MAKES A FAMILY

While love makes a family, those 1,138+ rights help keep that family together. Families with same-sex parents need to have access to the same rights and benefits as opposite-sex parents, including the right to file as head of household, the right to claim dependents, the right to pick up the kids from school, and to have family health insurance for dependents. Denying LGBT people these rights will not stop LGBT people from reproducing, nor will it stop them from loving their children or their partners. What it will do—and what it currently does—is subject these loving families to additional hardships that multiply under the already stressful realities of parenting.

seventeen

Retirement Homes
and Divorce Court

"Most elderly gay people live alone, and those who have lost a partner do not receive their partner's Social Security benefits, pension plans, or other inheritance rights—creating a serious vulnerability for them." —Terry Kaelber, executive director, Senior Action in a Gay Environment (SAGE)

Let's face it: One day we're all going to be old and gay! I know losing your hair, teeth, memory, and especially your sense of humor and fashion, seems extremely threatening, but that isn't the half of it! As we age we become more dependent on others. Eventually most of us will need some assistance with our everyday activities and may need to relocate to a retirement or assisted living home.

OK, so no big deal. After all, who wouldn't want to have access to those great buffets with the never-ending supply of rainbow-colored Jell-O? Maybe some of you Midwesterners or Jell-O addicts are smacking your lips just waiting for that day. Someone else to take care of the cooking, cleaning, laundry, toileting—overall it sounds like a great deal.

But don't forget to read the fine print on the brochures of some retirement homes. Many are run by religious organizations and have rules about unmarried people living together. They even discriminate against cohabiting heterosexual seniors, forcing the sinners to marry or get out. And while opposite-sex seniors *have* the option to marry, gay and lesbian seniors do not.

"Our income lowers as we age, and Social Security is our major form of retirement. However, LGBT people are not eligible to receive spousal benefits because we don't fit the marriage framework. Pension and 401K plans often don't recognize a surviving same-sex partner as a beneficiary. Same-sex couples often can't get health insurance either. Marriage ensures that spouses receive benefits that right now LGBT people can't get. I was in a heterosexual marriage that wasn't all that great. I've been reluctant to embrace the Freedom to Marry movement, but I've been rethinking that because domestic partnerships are so tenuous. I'm understanding what it means to have federal recognition for our community. I think we can rise to the challenge and create marriages in ways that make sense to us." —Joyce Pierson, head of the Elder Law Project for the National Center for Lesbian Rights

WHO ARE THE REAL SINNERS?

Juanita, my grandmother-in-law, moved in with a charming gent a couple of years after the death of her second husband. After being widowed twice, getting married at 89 seemed like more trouble than it was worth. She wanted company, but if things didn't go well, she didn't want to lose her survivor's pension from her deceased spouse. She decided to just move in with her new boyfriend. Well, it wasn't more than a month of seeing his car parked in her driveway that the "morality police" came knocking on her door. She was told that she either had to marry her new beau or she would have to leave the retirement community where she had lived for more than 10 years, a community she had served by teaching fitness classes, winning the green-thumb award for her gardening, and being a great friend to the people who lived there. So Grandma Juanita packed up her stuff and moved to a private house!

As it stands, many retirement homes force seniors to conform to their definition of family. According to the Lesbian and Gay Retirement Communities Web site (www.employees.org/-toal/gayaging/gayretirement/index.html), there are currently only six LGBT retirement communities in the United States—and none of them offer skilled care. SAGE Executive Director Terry Kaelber says gay seniors are more likely to live alone in old age and "less likely to have ties to a biological family or a religious institution." This makes them more likely to rely on existing retirement and care services. Yet because they are gay, they are less likely to be welcome to use these services. According to the National Gay and Lesbian Task Force (NGLTF), a 1994 study found that almost 50% of area agencies on aging (AAAs) would not want LGBT people at their centers. NGLTF notes that AAAs "provide the bulk of federally supported social services."

Imagine what it's like for Dolores and Fran. They've been together for 45 years and own a home together. Together they raised Dolores's children from a previous marriage and have taken care of each other through thick and thin. Now Dolores's health is declining, and her medical needs and personal assistance are more than what Fran can handle on her own. What's worse is that the quality of care Dolores will receive may be influenced by the homophobia of her providers. According to Terry Kaelber, in one facility a woman was left lying in her own filth because an aide refused to "wash the lesbian."

Dolores and Fran begin looking into retirement communities. Repeatedly, the two are given the message that two single ladies are not eligible to share a one-bedroom apartment. They can move in to the retirement community, but they will have to maintain separate residences, or at least rent a two-bedroom, which they can't afford and don't need. Maintaining separate residences is costly and unfair. It's as ridiculous as trying to squeeze into a twin bed at a hotel room, or pretending to have another bedroom to fool the company. Are same-sex partners supposedly to live in separate quarters in retirement homes—with one partner sneaking down the hall to the other partner's room? Come on!

The climate of intolerance and ignorance our transsexual elders must face is unfathomable. The Transgender Aging Network (TAN) is trying to address some of these issues and offers training and consultation services. "Many seniors feel the need to hide pictures and other signs of their gay identities, or their care will be compromised," notes Kaelber. And these seniors are not paranoid. An article from the Minnesota Board on Aging cited a study that found that "two thirds of doctors and medical students reported knowing of biased care giving by medical professionals; half reported witnessing it, and nearly 90% said they've heard disparaging remarks about GLBT patients."

> *"Members of the elderly lesbian and gay community experience a lot of frustration when they have to go to the hospital, or if they get a new nurse or physician. Having to continually explain who you are and what your relationship is to the person you are there with is demeaning. Instead of dealing with that, they often just stay away from care."* —Stephen Karpiak, Ph.D., executive director of the Pride Senior Network

Will we someday have to hide ourselves? Will we have to limit contact with our partners to ensure that we are not provided substandard medical care? Will we someday not be given medical care at all?

THE RIGHT TO DIVORCE!

Just as people never see themselves living in retirement homes, most newly committed couples don't imagine themselves breaking up and fighting over household items, cars, mortgages, pets, and children. While we know that more than 50% of American heterosexual marriages end in divorce, it is unclear how many same-sex committed relationships are terminated. The corollary to the right to marry is the right to divorce. Hey, I mean it. Go ahead: Tell me that when gays go through a breakup, everything is just sweetness and light—LGBT partners are so happy to divvy up the furniture, CDs, dishware, and money. Face it, when breaking up, human beings are never at their best. They fight over who paid for what, and what belongs to whom. Some wounded individuals tear all the photos in half and shout, "There! You can have your half of them!" And so on...

Yet most couples—including LGBT couples—don't want to spend a whole lot of time thinking "what if?" It takes away from the romance.

But what if you *do* find yourself in the middle of an ugly split-up? And what if your wife or husband is an attorney who also knows at least 20 family lawyers personally. You may not get the best end of the deal.

We've all heard the horror stories: the partner who was kicked to the curb; the partner who moved out but didn't get a penny from the sale of the house; the partner who stayed home and took care of the kids, pets, house, and whatever else while the other partner was bringing home the bread—suddenly, they all find themselves out in the cold without any savings, job, or home.

Take the case of Floridian Peggy Hammond. Hammond, a social worker, was in a 21-year relationship with her partner, a physician. The two women raised their adopted daughter together from her birth. However, because Florida law does not allow same-sex partners to adopt, only Peggy's partner's name was on the birth certificate. (The adoption would have been denied had her partner's sexuality been revealed at the time, because Florida law does not allow gay people to adopt period!)

The couple lived together for 21 years, raised their daughter, and accumulated several properties together, some owned jointly and some—including the house they shared—only in Peggy's partner's name. "We moved around a lot for her career since she was a doctor and made more money," Peggy explained. "I had to start over every time, and at the time we were buying the house they said we needed a jumbo loan, and they told her it would be difficult to get a mortgage with me. They said 'It's easier to do it this way.' "

Obviously, this shortcut was not easier in the long run. Peggy recalls that her partner "left one day in May 2002, without notice and moved in with a woman she had been having an affair with. Our daughter and I continued to live at the house. I tried to get her to settle our financial stuff. She said, 'You can have $100,000 and one of our properties. Take it or leave it.' We owned four properties together and had a child. That was not a fair agreement."

Peggy decided to pursue litigation, but that only made things worse. "I was in Vermont for a few weeks, when she was served with the papers. When I returned home, they (her ex-partner and her new lover) had moved back into the house and changed the locks." Then they came and took her daughter who, according to Peggy, told her, "Mom, I want people to hear my story. I have no rights here to choose who I want to live with. If you were married, I could at least choose."

Peggy had to get a court order to get into her house and pick up her belongings. Can you imagine anything more inflammatory? Your spouse of 21 years—for whom you've made enormous personal sacrifices—cheats on you, moves out with her mistress, then returns with her mistress and kicks you out of your home. In so doing, your former spouse denies you access to your clothes, furniture, and other belongings. She also denies you the right to see your child, takes away your financial resources, and then forces you to go to court to get your stuff back. Now that takes the wedding cake!

Because the state of Florida and the U.S. government does not allow gay people to adopt nor same-sex couples the right to marry, people like Peggy and her daughter will continue to suffer without the legal protections of divorce.

HERS AND HERS/HIS AND HIS

Marriage contracts in California and some other states give heterosexuals access to community property laws that assist in the division of their shared assets. Community property laws in marriage ensure that everything each partner owns belongs equally to both partners, investments and sacrifices made for the future being counted into the equation.

Let's say Jerome and Nick were able to legally marry and resided in a community property state such as California. If their relationship ended, their assets and property would at least be subject to guidelines to facilitate an equitable distribution.

It's bad enough figuring out which parent Fifi the French

poodle is going with, but custody wars over children are a nightmare. We've all seen perfectly sane and nice-seeming individuals sacrifice the good of an entire community just to get back at a partner in a soured relationship.

The only way to guarantee that LGBT people can have equal access to fairness in their breakups is for same-sex partners to have access to the laws and mediators that have been provided to heterosexual married couples. The only way to get that access is to grant same-sex couples the right to marry.

eighteen

Alien
Lovers

"Each year, federal law forces thousands of same-sex couples to break up or live in constant fear of deportation." —Human Rights Campaign press release, July 31, 2003

"After I was laid off at my dot-com, I had 10 days to find a job or be deported. My partner could not sponsor me." —Marta Donarye, cofounder of Love Sees No Borders

When Manuel's work visa expired he had two options: (1) leave Richard—the man he loved and had been with for the past four years of his life—and return to a country with a proud history of severe violence toward gay men or (2) stay illegally. Obviously, taking Richard back to live with his family was not an option.

Alice and Sarah had a similar story. The two met at the San Francisco Art Institute while Sarah was a visiting student from France. Sarah had wanted to stay on after she graduated but was unable to obtain residency or citizenship through her relationship with Alice. She felt her only option was to marry an American man. Sarah thought she understood the potential danger of her decision and didn't think it was a big deal. It wasn't until she was serving time in prison that she "got" the implications of the fraudulent marriage. Because they could not be legally married, Alice was not able to have conjugal visits with Sarah, and Sarah was to be deported after she served her sentence.

According to the Human Rights Campaign, "Approximately 75% of the 1 million green cards, or immigrant visas, issued each year go to family members of U.S. citizens and permanent residents." Gays and lesbians, however, are excluded from sponsoring their same-sex partners because the Immigration and Nationality Act does not recognize such relationships, making immigration status one of the most pressing issues in the lives of same-sex binational couples.

None of the domestic partnership or civil union legislation has provisions for sponsoring the immigration of a partner. Heterosexual marriage is the only vehicle that bestows this right.

"I'M NOT IN LOVE WITH AN IMMIGRANT, SO WHY SHOULD I CARE?"

Because if you're a gay or lesbian American, you are being denied a right that all heterosexual Americans have. Maybe you don't need that right, right now. But you can't predict whether you're going to fall in love with Molly from Minnesota or Maria from Mexico.

Most of the U.S. citizens I know who are in binational relationships didn't plan on falling in love with a non-U.S. citizen; it just happened. They didn't plan on having their lives complicated by the mess of immigration issues and marriage discrimination they currently face. Just ask Marta Donayre and Leslie Bulbuk, who started Love Sees No Borders, a nonprofit organization to address these concerns. The two met at a party, fell in love, and moved in together. Shortly after the dot-com crash, Marta was laid off. She was told she had 10 days to find new employment or she would be deported. Leslie was shocked by the possibility. This was the woman she planned to spend the rest of her life with. Marta was terrified of returning to her homophobic country, where gay people were in physical danger. She had to file for asylum, an emotionally grueling process.

AN AMERICAN LESBIAN IN LONDON

What happens when a woman travels overseas, meets the person of her dreams, and wants to bring that person back to America? If she's heterosexual, she'll have to fill out some paperwork, but ultimately she'll be able to do it. If she's a lesbian, her partner will have to apply for a work visa, and they'll both have to keep praying it will be renewed or that some nice employer will sponsor her for citizenship. Otherwise, her partner will be forced to either return to her own country or may—in her desperation—enter into a fraudulent heterosexual marriage which will grant her citizenship rights. If she pulls it off, she can stay. If she gets caught, it's prison, then deportation.

DOMESTIC PARTNERSHIP OR DEPORTATION?

What happens when a gay foreigner falls in love with an American citizen during his stay and wants to register as a domestic partner or get a Vermont civil union? Well, unlike the case with his heterosexual counterparts, it spells trouble—and may lead to deportation. Marta Donayre of Love Sees No Borders says that for the non-American partner in a same-sex binational couple, entering into any kind of legal same-sex relationship is a dangerous move.

The Immigration and Naturalization Service (INS) can deport a person who is here on a nonimmigrant visa and has "an intent to stay." According to Belinda Ryan and Wendy Daw of Immigration Equality, the INS is the subject of many horror stories for binational couples.

BELIEVE IT OR NOT!

A couple on a road trip within the United States are stopped at a random checkpoint 60 miles from the U.S.-Mexico border and asked to produce their passports. Because the noncitizen partner does not have his passport on him, even though he and his partner never left the country, he is detained at the local jail and then moved to several INS facilities for days until he is finally able to get in touch with his attorney, who helps to free him.

Back on holiday, after a lovely trip to Europe to visit the in-laws, a binational lesbian couple holding hands are stopped by a U.S. Customs agent at the airport. The agent informs her supervisor, who determines that the European partner is at risk for "overstay" and detains her. The U.S. woman is unable to remain with her partner, who is then deported immediately.

INTERROGATED FOR HOURS

Daniel and Ronnie know well the sting of marriage discrimination. Every time they cross the U.S.-Canadian border, Ronnie is subjected to hours of interrogation and intimidation. It started when he misplaced his return ticket and bought a roundtrip ticket because it was on sale and cheaper than the one-way fare. Immigration officials found this suspicious, so they held him for questioning for two-and-a-half hours, during which time his relationship with David came up. The immigration official was disturbed by Ronnie's admission of being involved in a "homosexual relationship" and denied him entry to the United States unless he could prove that his official residency was in his country of origin, Canada.

Ronnie returned with the documents, pay stubs, and electric bills, and was finally admitted into the United States. However, since that incident, he is stopped for several hours every time the couple crosses the border, often missing connecting flights. Did the homophobic immigration agent tag Ronnie as a security threat?

Most people don't plan for any kind of crisis, but binational same-sex couples have to live with all of these potential hardships and nightmares—all because they cannot legally marry. Many gay immigrants who cannot extend their visas or get citizenship choose to remain in the U.S. illegally, rather than leave their significant other. They then cannot return to their country of origin—even for a family funeral—because they would not be able to reenter the U.S.

EXILED FOR LOVE

The United States lags behind in immigration status. To date, at least 16 countries recognize same-sex couples for the purposes of immigration, but only Canada enables non-Canadians to make use of its laws, allowing binational couples from other countries to seek residency there. The other 15 countries require that at least one member of the couple be a citizen of their country. Countries that currently recognize same-sex couples' relationship status for immigration are:

Australia
Belgium

Brazil
Canada
Denmark
Finland
France
Germany
Iceland
Israel
The Netherlands
New Zealand
Norway
South Africa
Sweden
The United Kingdom

Many of these countries also provide some form of civil union or domestic partnership status as well. But why should Wendy have to permanently leave her family, her career, her friends, and her country just to be with her partner, Belinda? Why should she have to choose between her rights as a U.S. citizen or her right to be with the woman she loves?

And what if her brother had been the one who'd traveled to Europe and fallen in love with a charming girl from Wales?

ENTRY DENIED

Because Canada actively seeks immigrants, it makes it somewhat easier for same-sex partners to relocate there and start a new life together. But not everyone is welcomed with open arms. Canada is seeking professionals and skilled immigrants. Folks without any kind of higher education or professional training are not accepted. Bill the bartender and Roberto the busboy are just plain out of luck.

Canada also requires that applicants make a hefty deposit in a Canadian bank. Marriage discrimination hurts everyone, from every class background and racial and ethnic group, but it is particularly harsh on people with lower incomes.

"In addition to having a desired set of skills, Canada wants you to have a substantial amount of money in the bank so you can pay for your expenses until you find a job. You need to have 10,000 Canadian dollars per applicant plus 2,000 Canadian dollars per dependent. Since same-sex couples need to apply independently at first (if one is denied residency, then the relationship is looked at), this means that each couple would have to come up with at least 20,000 Canadian dollars before they can even start thinking about crossing the border." —Marta Donayre

Most Couples Don t Plan On:

¥Spending most of their savings on attorneys fees just so one partner can stay in the U.S. as long as possible, while simultaneously spending money to secure other options in Canada or one of the other countries that might recognize their relationship for immigration purposes.

¥Living their lives in complete uncertainty about what country they might be living in the next month.

¥ Being deported for a simple traffic violation.

Donayre also warns that this money does not include moving costs, or residency application costs, which are of $2,000 per person, suggesting that the average couple wishing to immigrate to Canada must have access to between $30,000 to $45,000 Canadian dollars to really be able to make the move.

THE PERMANENT PARTNERS IMMIGRATION ACT

"Our immigration laws treat gays and lesbians in committed relationships as second-class citizens, and that needs to change." —U.S. senator, Patrick Leahy, Democrat of Vermont, sponsor of the Permanent Partners Immigration Act

While we wait for the federal government to end its reign of discrimination against LGBT citizens, one hope does exist for American citizens in a binational relationship. If Congress and the Senate approve a new bill called the Permanent Partners Immigration Act (Senate bill 1510 and HR-832), U.S. citizens would be allowed to sponsor their same-sex partners. According to Immigration Equality, the PPIA would modify the federal Immigration and Nationality Act, adding the "term 'permanent partner' to the federal law's list of definitions of family" and providing "same-sex partners of U.S. citizens and same-sex partners of lawful permanent residents the same immigration rights that legal spouses of U.S. residents enjoy." As of November 2003, the bill has only 119 cosponsors. Please see Appendix A for information on how you can help pass this bill.

HOSPITALITY VERSUS HOSTILITY

"Each arriving traveler or responsible family member must provide the following information (only

ONE *written declaration per family is required)."*
—U.S. Customs form

In September 2003, Joe Varnell and his husband, Kevin Bourassa, a legally married couple from Canada, were traveling to Georgia on vacation when a U.S. customs official stopped them in line, demanding that they fill out two separate forms and mark "single" under their marital status. The couple was outraged and explained that they were Canadians who were legally married in their country and had every right to check the "married" box and fill out one form as the instructions indicated. The official then informed them that "the United States does not recognize same-sex marriages!" and that they would have to comply with his request if they wanted to enter the country.

Joe and Kevin decided to cancel their vacation instead.

"It's an invasion of the charter rights and values that we have in our country. We simply ask that the United States recognize a marriage that their neighbors to the north do. A little piece of our dignity has been chipped away."
—Kevin Bourassa

Four congresspeople responded to this outrageous Customs decision and sent the following letter to the U.S. Customs commissioner. However, it is unclear if anything will be done to change this homophobic policy. When I called the White House comments line to complain about it, I was lectured by the receptionist and given the same ignorant response Kevin and Joe received.

"The United States does not recognize same-sex marriages!"

Until it does, legally married same-sex couples will continue to be treated in an undignified and hostile manner, in direct contrast to the respect and deference afforded all other foreign families who enter our country.

October 1, 2003
The Honorable Robert C. Bonner
Commissioner
U.S. Customs Service
1300 Pennsylvania Avenue, N.W.
Washington, D.C. 20229

Dear Mr. Commissioner,

We were very disappointed to read that Customs officials refused to allow a same-sex Canadian couple to enter the U.S. as long as they insisted on writing their Canadian marital status on their entry card. We are aware that a section of American law prohibits the American government from recognizing same-sex marriages. Regardless of the merits of that law, we do not believe that this law compels the result that happened in this case. Had the two men been allowed to enter the U.S. with their Canadian marital status listed on the form, they would have been entitled to no legal rights or privileges in the U.S. as a married couple. Nothing legal in the sense that the statute governs would have been affected had their declaration that they were a Canadian married couple been honored. We should note that many of us would like to change this, but at this time it is the existing policy.

We do not understand why it should be American policy to insist that people seeking to enter our country as tourists from another country repudiate their own country's rules and engage in what are to them wholly inaccurate self descriptions, and in a way that they understandably found to be degrading. Forcing people to deny their own important values, when this has no legal bearing in the U.S., serves no valid public purpose, and whatever its motivation, becomes a form of meanness—inflicting emotional pain on people for no reason other than to express our official disapproval of them. We urge you to reverse this policy.

Signed by representatives Sheila Jackson Lee of Texas, the senior Democrat on the Judiciary Committee Subcommittee on Immigration, Border Security, and Claims; Loretta Sanchez of California, the senior Democrat on the Homeland Security Committee Subcommittee on Infrastructure and Border Security; Jerrold Nadler of New York, the senior Democrat on the Judiciary Committee Subcommittee on the Constitution; and Barney Frank of Massachusetts, the senior Democrat on the Financial Services Committee.

nineteen

Transsexual
Issues

"My partner is transgendered. She has not had sex reassignment surgery because of a medical condition but has changed her name and identity for over 20 years. I don't think she can marry anyone legally."
—Marriage Equality activist and partner of a female transsexual

According to NCLR—who provided Mr. Kantaras's legal representation—the *Kantaras v. Kantaras* case (2000) was "the first in the country to determine whether a transgender man has the right to marry and be a parent." Michael Kantaras was born female but underwent sexual reassignment surgery in 1987. He met his wife, Linda, two years later, and told her he was a transsexual before she married him. They were married for nine years and raised two children together. Although Linda had always known Michael was a transsexual, during the divorce proceedings she still asked the court to invalidate their marriage and to deny Michael any parental rights solely because he was not a "real man." Ouch! Luckily, the court ruled that Michael was the better parent and should have primary custody. (It should also be noted that, according to insiders, Linda's decisions were influenced by her local minister.)

WELCOME TO LEGAL LIMBO LAND!

When it comes to marriage rights, transsexual men and women in this country have an even more complicated road to traverse.

For example, in California, transitioned female-to-male (FTM) or male-to-female (MTF) people are able to legally marry partners of a different sex. But these marriages can still be challenged at probate or in the courts. Transitioned MTF's can legally marry only males; pre-transition MTF's can legally marry only females. So, at least in California, a lesbian born with male genitals would do well to marry her female partner before her transition. After her transition, she would be able to marry only a man.

LEGAL GAY MARRIAGE IN TEXAS AND KANSAS?

A Texas appellate court invalidated a marriage of seven years between a female, Christine Littelton, and her deceased husband. The same thing happened to J'Noel Gardiner in Kansas when the court ruled for the deceased's contesting child, on the grounds that "a person's legal sex is genetically fixed at birth." This ruling denied the widow's access to Social Security benefits, the right to inheritance without a will, the right to sue for wrongful death, the right to retirement benefits, other survivorship benefits, and the dignity and respect normally afforded a grieving widow.

Because of these decisions, FTMs and MTFs in Texas and Kansas are not legally recognized as having changed their sex. No matter how much they spend on surgery, name changes, and so on, they cannot marry people of their previous gender. In other words, a transitioned gay man or lesbian *can* legally marry his or her partner; heterosexuals cannot. And so, through an ignorance-based loophole, Kansas and Texas are the only states that actually allow a form of same-sex marriage. Let's not all move there at once.

Following the Littleton ruling in Texas, two women, one of them an MTF, applied for and obtained a marriage license in San Antonio. In an article titled "Lesbian Wedding Allowed in Texas by Gender Loophole," Jessica and Robin Wicks discussed picking up their license. "We know we love each other, and in a real sense we're already married in our hearts, but there's something about the piece of paper that says this is the way it should be." According to the article, Republican Texas state representative Arlene Wohlgemuth asserted, "We don't object to a marriage license being issued, since we do favor a marriage between a man and woman and this fits the legal definition of gender." Huh?

Dianne Hardy-Garcia, former executive director of the Lesbian/Gay Rights Lobby of Texas, maintained that the Littleton decision shows the ridiculousness of current laws. "Marriage is a private matter," she said. "I don't think the state has any business defining who should be able to get married between consenting adults."

The couple's attorney, Phyllis Randolph Frye, hopes other transsexual people will travel to San Antonio and get married.

EVERYWHERE ELSE

According to Shannon Minter of NCLR, "The legal validity of marriage involving a transsexual spouse is not yet firmly established in most states. Some states may allow FTM or MTF transsexuals to marry their now opposite-sex spouses, but the legality of the marriages may be contested later in court, as with the Kantaras case in

Florida. Only New Jersey and Florida have cases that recognize the marriage of a person as valid when contested in
court. Because of this, Minter urges couples where one
partner is transsexual to create written documentation
that includes "wills of both partners, financial and medical
powers of attorney, a written personal relationship agreement including a detailed account of each spouse's rights
and responsibilities with regard to finances, property, support, children, and other issues that are important to the
couple." Minter also emphasizes that such an agreement
should also contain an acknowledgment that the non-
transsexual partner is aware that his or her spouse is transsexual.

Using an attorney to do the above is advised.

I can only imagine what it must be like to be legally
married in New Jersey but unable to move to Utah because
your marriage may be contested or rendered null and void.
So much for the equal protection clause!

LIVING OUTSIDE THE BOX

Many transsexuals are at varying levels of transition.
Some will never choose full surgery because of the
expense, health concerns, or many other personal reasons.
Because they are not legally seen as having had a sex reassignment, these people are denied the rights of marriage
pertaining to a person of their self-identified sex.

According to transsexual activist Owen Wolf,
"Whether one can change one's sex—surgery or not—
depends on where the transsexual is born. Birth certificates
can be changed in California with one surgery, in some
states with all possible surgeries for the appropriate sex
being assumed, and cannot be changed in some other
states regardless of surgery. *No state allows a transsexual
to declare themselves to be of the other sex without sur-*

gery, even if surgery is not needed (such as in the case of an FTM with minimal breasts) or contraindicated due to other health issues such as heart condition or diabetes."

The adoption of full marriage equality would provide all transsexual adults—regardless of sexual orientation and regardless of level of transition—equal participation in the institution of marriage.

One transsexual woman advised me that she really wanted to marry her same-sex partner, whom she met after her reassignment. She had never had "the surgery" because of a medical condition, and she wondered if she might be able to marry her partner. If she was able to do this, would it require her to use a "long dead male identity"? This woman really wanted to marry her lover but was reluctant to bring someone back to life who'd essentially been "dead" for 20 years. "I would not be able to stand having that reminder of such a painful part of my life on such a sacred and meaningful document as our marriage certificate," she said, "and my partner would not feel right with it either."

INTERSEXUAL RIGHTS

"Not everyone is born with a set of chromosomes, XX or XY, that clearly defines gender. Hermaphrodite and other cases of confused genetics could pose problems."
—Jack Sampson, University of Texas law professor, in reference to the Littleton case

"The law, by clinging to a binary system that blindly denies the existence of intersexuals and the importance of self-identity, reinforces the perception that intersexuality is unacceptable." —Julie Greenberg, San Diego Thomas Jefferson School of Law

According to the Intersex Society of North America (ISNA), "Intersex" refers to variations of genital and/or reproductive anatomy, and these occur in approximately one in 1,500 births. Being intersexed is simply an anatomical variation—just like hair and skin color. However, some intersexed individuals may have serious medical and endocrinological conditions that require treatment.

It is unclear how the laws of the marriage game relate to intersexed folks. There are no known marriage cases in which intersexed people have challenged the courts for the right to marry based on chromosomal status. National Center for Lesbian Rights attorney Karen Doering noted that the courts in the Littleton and Gardiner cases in Texas and Kansas presumed that the women were both chromosomally XY, however, to her knowledge, genetic testing was not done. Therefore, the courts determined that genetics determined sex, which determined marriage rights.

But what about cases in which someone is born XXY? Doering noted that a genetic presentation of XXY prompted Olympic officials to disqualify a female athlete, stating that she was male for purposes of competition—even though she later gave birth to a child. What would have happened if this athlete had tried to marry a woman? What would happen now if an XXY tried to marry an XX?

What determines sex or gender is more complicated than our binary system allows. Intersexed individuals are forced into boxes they don't fit into. Under the current law, a person with an XXY makeup should be able to legally marry either sex because they are chromosomally both. Either way you look at the situation, the person would be in a heterosexual marriage.

CHILDREN OF HERMES

What about the infant who is forced into sex reassignment surgery before his or her identity even has a chance to develop?

Kim was born with ovaries and a penis. When she was still just a baby, her parents decided that she would be Ken, their little boy. Ken, however, never felt comfortable as a boy and often wore dresses and makeup, and by the time he was 14 he ran away from home and lived on the streets, where he felt he could be himself. He began working as a prostitute at an early age to be able to provide for himself and to pay for hormone therapy.

After surgery, Kim finally emerged. Much to the chagrin of doctors who'd hoped the sex change would "normalize" Ken, Kim—whose body contained both male and female organs—was bisexual. Why should Kim and others like her be denied the opportunity to marry either sex?

twenty

Choose:
Your Country
or Your Family?

"The military is still a breeding ground for nastiness against gays. You can still say 'f*ck you fag!' at work and get away with it!" —Jody Hoenninger, Servicemembers Legal Defense Network.

"Moral disapproval of a group does not justify discrimination." —Supreme Court Decision *Lawrence v. Texas*, 2003

"I loved the camaraderie, integrity and challenge of the military environment. But I could not continue to live a lie and put my family in jeopardy by staying in the service." —Abbie Sommer, former Air Force sergeant

Here is a quandary many young soldiers have faced: You join the military at age 20 looking for an adventurous career and an opportunity to serve your country. Three years into your military service, you meet and fall in love with a person of the same sex. Uh-oh! You love your job, you have excelled and received recognition from your superiors for

171

outstanding service. You make a good wage, have great benefits, and can see yourself staying in the military for the rest of your career, except for one important fact.

You are gay.

After all, the military is the largest employer native to America, and still offers some of the best available jobs if you are trying to get out of your small town. Not only does a military career pay comparatively well, but just four years of service comes with tremendous benefits for education, on-the-job training during your enlistment, and VA loans after you separate. Military service is a great place to begin if you don't have the money to put yourself through college or need additional discipline and structure to get you going. But the Catch-22 is that you can't protect your country and your family at the same time!

YOU CAN'T PROTECT YOUR FAMILY IF YOU CAN'T SERVE OPENLY

A wounded gay or lesbian service member is forbidden from turning to a fellow soldier and asking, "Please, call my partner and let him know I'm OK." The service member cannot have a picture of a same-sex partner in a wallet, can't make phone calls to the partner, can't tell anyone anything about his or her partner—let alone access any of the benefits provided to military families, including housing.

Since the implementation of the "don't ask, don't tell" policy, service members will be removed from the military if they are identified as associated with anything gay. Many people don't realize how inhumane "don't ask, don't tell" is; they simply see it as a directive for gays not to flaunt their sexual orientation. Nothing could be farther from the truth. According to Jody Hoenninger of the Servicemembers Legal Defense Network, "The only part of the 'don't ask, don't tell' policy that is enforced is 'don't tell.' "LGBT service members' private lives are constantly scrutinized, including people reading their diaries, letters, and computer files, and viewing their personal photos. "A service member must even think twice about whom he designates as a beneficiary on his insurance policy," Hoenninger says.

THE THREAT IS REAL

According to statistics compiled by Servicemembers Legal Defense Network, *3 to 4 service members are discharged every day* because of "don't ask, don't tell." Since the policy's implementation in 1993, taxpayers have paid more than $230 million to carry it out. The military spends millions in advertising to recruit new members—and spends even more millions kicking out hundreds of recruits every year. And it's not because they're doing an inadequate job.

Even though the Supreme Court struck down all state criminal sodomy laws in *Lawrence v. Texas*, the military retains the power to set its own rules. Section 125 of the Uniform Code of Military Justice continues to prohibit oral and anal sex—both homosexual and heterosexual. General Articles 133 and 134 prohibit an even broader range of sexual and affectionate conduct. The only lesbians or gay men permitted to stay in the military are those who don't have sex or committed relationships. I wonder how many heterosexual soldiers would be willing to serve under that condition. The irony is that the government mandates that all gay and lesbian soldiers remain celibate and partnerless, while their heterosexual partners marry, remarry, cheat, and paint the town red in every port.

Despite the fact that U.S. service members serve alongside troops from Great Britain, Israel, Canada, Czech Republic, Sweden, and other countries that do not discriminate against gay and lesbian service members, without incident, the policy remains in place. Currently, U.S. service members may be investigated and administratively discharged if they:

1. Make a statement that they are lesbian, gay, or bisexual
2. Engage in physical contact with someone of the same sex for the purposes of sexual gratification; or
3. *Marry or attempt to marry, someone of the same sex.*
[Dept. of Defense Directive No. 1332.14]

Even if same-sex couples *were* able to obtain marriage licenses in the United States, LGBT service members would not be able to marry a member of the same sex and continue to serve in the military. If the service member were to marry, or if he or she entered into a domestic partnership or civil union, it would still be deemed a violation of the policy and grounds for immediate discharge.

THIS IS HOW IT LOOKS:

Mindy has been in a relationship with her partner, Ana, for several years. Ana is career military. Lately the two have been struggling about how to protect themselves financially as their lives become more intertwined. Because Amy is in the military, she cannot put Mindy on the deed of the house she bought with VA loans before she met Mindy. If Ana were to put Mindy on the deed, she would be immediately discharged! Because of this, Mindy is left unprotected. She lives in a house she does not own, and if anything were to happen to Ana, she could lose her home to Ana's so-called next of kin. Mindy would be left with nothing, despite having helped with the mortgage payments for the seven years she and Ana have lived together.

Ana is afraid that even if she draws up a will, power of attorney, or a medical directive, her relationship will become known and will violate the "don't ask, don't tell" policy. Therefore, none of her assets are earmarked to Mindy. If Ana dies serving her country, not only will Mindy not get any of her death benefits, (i.e. life insurance, eligibility for VA loans, pension, family grief counseling, etc.), she will also not be entitled to any of the assets she and Ana built up—the furniture, the cars, the house, and so on. In fact, Mindy would have to produce receipts indicating what belongings are hers. Otherwise, Ana's next of kin, (who could be a third cousin Ana never met) will legally be entitled to Ana and Mindy's shared property.

Even though Ana and Mindy live in California, a state that offers domestic partnership registration, they cannot register as domestic partners; otherwise, Ana could be discharged from the military. If either Mindy or Ana were to become ill to the point of a life-threatening situation, neither partner would have hospital visitation or medical decision-making rights.

PARTNERS MUST BE SILENT OR FACE DISCHARGE

Let me tell you the real-life story of Air Force Captain Monica Hill. A few days before Monica was scheduled to report to Andrews Air Force Base, she learned that Terri, her partner of 14 years, had been diagnosed with brain cancer. Monica was confronted with having to request a deferment from her commanding officers so that she could care for Terri. When pressed for a reason for the deferment, Monica had to choose between telling a lie or telling the truth.

Monica told the truth.

Her commanding officer initiated discharge proceedings.

Less than two months after her partner's death, Monica was interviewed as part of the discharge proceedings. She produced Terri's death certificate and the signed rental contract for the apartment where she and Terri had intended to reside off base. Nevertheless, the interviewing officer insinuated that in revealing her sexual orientation Monica was only trying to get out of completing her service commitment. The Air Force demanded that Monica repay the U.S. government for all of her medical school tuition.

GAY VETS

Many LGBT people have already served this country. Yet these same men and women who have put their lives on the line have not been given equal status back home. There is no justice in this second-class citizenship. Why should Dan, a Vietnam Vet, not be able to share his pension and health benefits with his loving partner, Jake? Why should Elida, a military nurse exposed to Agent Orange during the Vietnam War, not be able to share her benefits with her partner of 20 years?

Again, the innumerable rights granted by civil marriage become of prime importance. A whopping 270 of the 1,138 federal rights associated with marriage have to do with federal civilian and military service benefits.

NO COMMISSARY FOR YOU!

Once you leave military service, you are free to breathe and come out. But the time you spent serving your country doesn't entitle your partner to your veteran health benefits, commissary privileges, student loans, housing loans, or any of the sundry other rights afforded spouses of veterans.

Spouses of military service members are granted numerous privileges not afforded to other civilians, such as being able to shop at the tax-free commissary or buy gasoline on the base at a significantly reduced rate. Partners of LGBT service members are denied access to counseling, educational, and financial benefits including commissary benefits, death benefits, medical benefits, and veterans' preferences.

A special benefit for deployed service members are free phone calls back home. Gay service members obviously don't have this option. Opposite-sex spouses of service members deployed overseas are afforded special housing too. LGBT service members are denied all these benefits and more because they are forced to serve in silence—and since they cannot be legally wed.

> *"Unlike their heterosexual counterparts, gay service members who fall in love overseas will not be able to bring their partners back to the States."*
> **—Leslie Bulbuk, Love Sees No Borders**

twenty-one

20 Things You Can Do to Make a Difference

"Where we stand on civil rights is a test of who we are. We must be vigilant in our efforts to ensure that no one is a victim of discrimination due to sexual orientation. When we have amended the Constitution, it has been to expand people's rights." —Rep. Jane Harman, National Coming Out Day 2003

The phenomenon of straight folks enjoying *Boy Meets Boy, Will and Grace*, and *Queer Eye for the Straight Guy*, doesn't mean LGBT people have arrived any more than whites owning Sambo dolls and watching *Amos and Andy* signaled equal rights for African-Americans. Until LGBT people have full equality we will continue to be marginalized. We must stand up and be counted, and we must urge our non-gay allies to stand with us. We must demand respect and equal treatment. We must insist on being allowed to drink at the "marriage" water fountain and to refuse to get up from the "marriage" lunch counter until we are served. In the words of Marriage Equality: "Marriage, anything less is less than equal!"

> **The most obvious thing you can do to make a difference is to give this book to all your friends and family members.**

1. Come out to everyone! It's harder to discriminate against someone you know.

If you're straight, come out for full marriage equality for all couples. Talk about it at work, over lunch with friends, in your social circles, and in your churches, temples, and other organizations.

2. Have a wedding ceremony and invite everyone you know! Sure it's expensive, but it's worth the money and effort. Plus, you'll be surprised: People you'd think would politely decline will attend. After all, who *doesn't* want to say they've been to an alternative wedding ceremony? And when your guests come and see you and your new spouse gazing into each other's eyes, so deeply in love, their hearts may flutter a bit too.

If you're straight, mention the unfairness of denying same-sex couples the right to marry in all 50 states at your wedding ceremony. Mention those 1,138+ rights, so our guests know the real truth about tying the knot!

3. Let everyone know you're married! Put up wedding pictures in your office. Use the words *husband*, *wife*, and *spouse*. When filling out paperwork, claim the status "married" for yourselves (except on your state and federal tax forms). Before your ceremony use the words *fiancé*, *bride*, and *groom*. It will feel weird, but growth and change are like that.

"domestic partner," "civil union," and "legally married in another country" on forms and applications. This will spur interesting conversation between you and the receptionist or office manager and be a great opportunity to educate him or her about the inequities you (or your LGBT friends) face by not being able to legally marry. People don't need a lot of information to become sympathetic to our plight. For example, a simple verbal or written explanation about how you were legally married in Canada and returned to the U.S. as legal strangers (unable to visit your unconscious spouse in the hospital, let alone make medical decisions for him) will outrage many uninformed citizens.

5. Join an organization fighting for marriage equality. Start a Marriage Equality Chapter in your city or county. It's easy and fun! I've made so many incredible friends across the state and country through my marriage activism, whom otherwise I would have never had the opportunity to meet. (Now I have places to stay in all 50 states.)

You can also download Marriage Equality's sample "marriage declarations" and get people to sign them. The declarations are general enough that they can be tailored to specific situations in a different state or territory. Make copies of these declarations and send them to your city council members, mayor, assembly members, governor, U.S. representatives and senators, and the president.

6. Donate generously. Help out the organizations (a list is provided in the next section) who are fighting for marriage equality.

7. Organize meetings in your town to discuss same-sex marriage. Town Hall meetings worked well in Massachusetts and Vermont because they gave people a forum to dialogue about the issues and ask those burning questions that were too embarrassing to ask anywhere else.

8. Get local clergy organized on same-sex marriage. Convince socially progressive clergy and lay people to lead prayers for gays and lesbians to have equal rights. After years of hearing the old "love the sinner, hate the sin" refrain, and of having Bibles thumped in our faces, being blessed as we are can be a powerfully healing experience. You can also enlist clergy to write letters to elected officials, copies of which you can keep in a binder, along with other letters from LGBT people, couples, families and their straight allies. Compiling these binders and sending them out, or personally showing them, to your city council members, mayor, assembly members, representatives, senators, governor, and even president can help politicians see who we are and who they are hurting when they deny us equal rights.

9. Write letters to the editor. Explain the specific hardships you have faced by not being able to legally marry or share your best wedding memories. Letters that start out with "I love my husband because...." and then later surprise the readers with the gender of the spouse are my favorite. This approach can disarm people who feel that they can't relate to a gay person or a same-sex couple. Love is universal.

If you're not gay or lesbian, write about why you believe your friends should be able to legally marry.

10. Get your local media to do stories on same-sex marriage. Invite them to your ceremony. Have them follow you and a group of friends as you go to City Hall and ask for a marriage license. It's very compelling for people to see you being turned away—especially on camera. Viewers at home can have time to process their responses.

11. Go to City Hall and ask for a marriage license. Let people see how it feels to deny and be denied. It's one thing to know that you can't eat at the lunch counter, quite another to be told to leave or to be denied service.

Non-gay people should experience what antigay discrimination feels like, so take your straight friends with you as witnesses when you go to request a marriage license.

Asking for something and then being denied is a demoralizing and emotional experience. Straight friends can provide emotional support.

12. Become a part of a speakers' bureau and do outreach. The more people hear about how what same-sex couples go through, the more their hearts and minds are changed. In particular, young people of stripes tend to be supportive of same-sex marriage and LGBT civil rights. Idealism is a great thing! Non-gay allies make some of the best speakers on this subject because they aren't immediately discredited as sinners or as involved in the movement for reasons of personal gain. Also, marriage inequality is so painful for some LGBT people that it's too difficult to talk about while having to endure harsh criticism and personal attacks. Non-gay allies are less likely to take these comments personally.

13. Target your state's insurance commissioner. Locate the insurance commissioner in your state and inundate him or her with letters requesting that same-sex couples be provided the marriage discount on auto insurance. If the commissioner gives the excuse that discounts are based on "research," challenge him or her. Ask just what research, if any, has studied the risk factors for same-sex domestic partners having automobile accidents.

California residents should send correspondence to: California Department of Insurance, Consumer Communications Bureau, 300 S. Spring, South Tower, Los Angeles, CA 90013.

14. Send your wedding announcement to your local paper.

15. Vote for candidates who support civil unions or civil marriage for same-sex couples. Especially presidential candidates.

16. Get involved in the workplace Contact your human resource manager at work and find out what benefits you and your family are denied because you are not able to legally marry. Work to change these policies, thus making the workplace fair and equitable.

17. Get your city council members to pass resolutions in support of marriage equality. In California, resolutions supporting same-sex marriage have been passed in Santa Monica, Berkeley, San Francisco, Santa Cruz, and Davis.

18. Get local businesses to sign declarations in support of marriage equality and the Permanent Partners Immigration Act (PPIA).

19. Write your congressperson and ask him or her to:

- sign on to the Permanent Partners Immigration Act. See Appendix A.

- come out against the Federal Marriage Amendment. See Appendix B.
- repeal "don't ask, don't tell." See Appendix C.
- overturn the Defense of Marriage Act. See Appendix D.
- support domestic partnership benefits for federal employees. See Appendix E.

20. In the words of Jessie Jackson, "Keep hope alive!" Never stop believing that full and equal rights are attainable and that you can make a difference by speaking out and working to make this dream a reality. One day we *shall* overcome. Bear in mind how we can all look back on the days of segregation and antimiscegenation laws and wonder, *What was all the fuss about?* It took the commitment of many abolitionists, suffragists, and civil rights activists for justice to prevail. Likewise, as more of us are out there declaring equal rights and liberties for LGBT people, the faster an old chapter of discrimination will end and a new one full of hopes and promises will begin.

ORGANIZATIONS FIGHTING FOR MARRIAGE EQUALITY

Marriage Equality USA (MEUSA)
P.O. Box 121
Old Chelsea Station
New York, NY 10113-0121
(877) 571-5729 (phone and fax)
www.marriageequality.org

Marriage Equality New York (MENY)
P.O. Box 121
Old Chelsea Station
New York, NY 10113-0121

(877) 772-0089 (phone and fax)
www.marriageequalityny.org

Marriage Equality California (MECA)
P.O. Box 8
Venice, CA 90294
(877) 356-4125
www.marriageequalityca.org

Marriage Equality Texas (METX)
LGRL of Texas
P.O. Box 2340
Austin, TX 78768
(512) 474-5475 (phone)
(512) 474-6297 (fax)
www.lgrl.org/marriageequality/

Freedom to Marry
116 W. 23rd St., Suite 500
New York, NY 10011
(212) 851-8418 (phone)
(646) 375-2069 (fax)
www.freedomtomarry.org

Freedom to Marry Coalition Massachusetts
325 Huntington Ave, Suite 88
Boston, MA 02115-4401
www.equalmarriage.org

Freedom to Marry Coalition California
3325 Wilshire Blvd, Suite 130
Los Angeles, CA 90010-1729
(213) 247-0665
www.civilmarriage.org

Equality California
Northern California Office
2370 Market St.
San Francisco, CA 94114
(415) 581-0005 (phone)
(415) 581-0805 (fax)

Legislative Office
1127 11th St., Suite 208
Sacramento, CA 95812
(916) 554-7681 (phone)
(916) 914-2494 (fax)
www.eqca.org

Equality Florida
1222 S. Dale Mabry, #652
Tampa, FL 33629
(813) 870-3735 (phone)
(813) 870-1499 (fax)
www.eqfl.org

Basic Rights Oregon
P.O. Box 40625
Portland, OR 97240
(503) 222-6151 (phone)
(503) 236-6686 (fax)
www.basicrights.org

American Civil Liberties Union Lesbian and Gay Rights and AIDS Projects
125 Broad St., 18th Floor
New York, NY 10004
(212) 549-2627
www.aclu.org/getequal/contact.htm/

Don't Amend
www.dontamend.com

Equal Marriage for Same Sex Couples in Canada
Kevin Bourassa and Joe Varnell
c/o Bruce E. Walker Law Office
65 Wellesley St., E., Suite 205
Toronto, Ontario, Canada
M4Y1G7
(416) 961-7451
www.equalmarriage.ca
www.samesexmarriage.ca

Gay Civil Unions
www.gay-civil-unions.com

Gay & Lesbian Advocates and Defenders (GLAD)
30 Winter St., Suite 800
Boston, MA 02108
(617) 426-1350
www.glad.org

Human Rights Campaign
1640 Rhode Island Ave., N.W.
Washington, DC 20036
(202) 628-4160 (phone)
(202) 347-5323 (fax)
www.hrc.org

Immigration Equality (formerly The Lesbian & Gay Immigration Rights Task Force)
350 W. 31st St., Ste. 505
New York, NY 10001
(212) 714-2904

Lambda Legal Defense and Education Fund
National Headquarters
120 Wall St., Suite 1500
New York, NY 10005-3904
(212) 809-8585 (phone)
(212) 809-0055 (fax)
www.lambdalegal.org

Love Makes a Family
44 Wright Drive
Avon, Connecticut 06001
(860) 674-8942
www.lmfct.org

National Center for Lesbian Rights
870 Market St., Suite 570
San Francisco, CA 94102
(415) 392-6257 (phone)
(415) 392-8442 (fax)
www.nclrights.org

Partners Task Force for Gay and Lesbian Couples
www.buddybuddy.com

Bite-Size Activism Appendices

I have included five sample letters to senators or representatives that demonstrate how easy it is to be an activist and make a difference on this issue. Please take some time to read the letters. Type them up into your own computer, perhaps adding your own perspective for personal flair, and send them out.

Some people have Tupperware parties. Others, like me, have letter-writing parties. The letters don't have to be literary masterworks; it really is about quantity. Believe me, the fanatical Leviticus-reciting Bible-thumpers have been sending form letters en masse for decades. In the words of PFLAG Dad and democratic presidential candidate Dick Gephardt: "Politics is an alternative to violence."

Let's go get 'em!

Appendix A
Sample Letter to Senator in Support of the Permanent Partners Immigration Act

The Honorable Senator Feinstein
One Post Street, Suite 2450
San Francisco, CA 94104

Dear Senator Feinstein:

I am writing you today to ask you to sponsor the Permanent Partners Immigration Act (PPIA), S.1510. The Permanent Partners Immigration Act is a bill that seeks to amend the Immigration and Nationality Act by adding the term "permanent partner" where the word "spouse" currently appears.

As you may be aware, United States immigration law is based on the principle of "family reunification." Accordingly, it allows U.S. citizens to reunite with their parents, children, siblings, and spouses every day by sponsoring these "family" members for immigration. The law, however, does note recognize gay and lesbian families or grant the same sponsorship benefit to gay and lesbian U.S. citizens. There is no way that U.S. citizens can sponsor their same-sex or transsexual partners for immigration on the basis of their relationships. Consequently, thousands of lesbians and gay binational couples are kept apart, torn apart, or forced to live in fear of deportation. Love knows no borders, but immigration law is keeping us apart.

Sincerely,

YOUR NAME AND ADDRESS HERE

Appendix B
Sample Letter to Senator Against the Federal Marriage Amendment

The Honorable John Kerry
304 Russell Senate Office Building
Washington, DC 20510

Dear Senator Kerry:

As you may know, a mean-spirited bill has been introduced by Rep. Marilyn Musgrave, who wishes to change the U.S. Constitution to resemble her personal religious beliefs. The definitive fundamental texts of the United States are the Bill of Rights and the Declaration of Independence, and the law of this country is the Constitution, not the Bible. Yet many leaders feel compelled to force their religious beliefs on others, through faith-based government programs, school prayer, and now by attempting to rewrite the U.S. Constitution to include blatant discrimination. I am speaking about the Federal Marriage Amendment, which would change the Constitution to state that "marriage is between a man and a woman only," effectively denying same-sex couples access to more than 1,138 federal and state relationship rights, responsibilities, and protections, and any other form of relationship recognition. This amendment would also nullify existing domestic partnerships and civil unions and prevent states and local governments from passing any additional recognitions for same-sex couples as well as other cohabiting couples, such as seniors over 62, who now enjoy domestic partner rights in Ohio and California.

Never in the history of this country has the Constitution been changed to accommodate discrimination. To the contrary, the U.S. Constitution has been changed to provide for rights that had previously been denied to groups, such as the right for women to vote and to outlaw slavery. Ms. Musgrave's proposed amendment represents the view of a radical reactionary minority who seek to codify their religious beliefs into law and deny American citizens basic civil rights. If this bill passes, it will not only ban same-sex marriage, it will effectively deny gay, lesbian, bisexual, and transsexual people the most basic of relationship rights, including the right to visit a partner in the hospital during a life-threatening situation, the right to be recognized as next of kin, and the right to make medical decisions for a partner.

Despite Ms. Musgrave's failure to separate church from state, many religious communities do support the civil rights of same-sex couples to engage in meaningful relationships with equal legal rights and responsibilities. However, no religious denomination, regardless of its stance on blessings of same-sex couples, has the legal standing to confer those rights to same-sex couples because civil marriage is a contractual arrangement bound by civil law. America's neighbors to the north have realized that denying same-sex couples the right to marry is unconstitutional, as did the judges in the Hawaii, Vermont, and Massachusetts marriage cases. I urge you to uphold your oath and protect the U.S. Constitution against its enemies and to come out against the Federal Marriage Amendment.

Sincerely,

YOUR NAME AND ADDRESS HERE

Appendix C
Sample Letter to U.S. Representative Against "Don't Ask, Don't Tell"

Barney Frank
Congressman, 4th District, Massachusetts
Washington Office:
2252 Rayburn House Office Building
Washington, D.C. 20515

Dear Congressman Frank:

I am writing to urge you to insist that the Pentagon lift the ban on gay, bisexual, and lesbian members of the U.S. armed forces. According to statistics compiled by the Servicemembers Legal Defense Network, *three to four service members are discharged every day* under the "don't ask, don't tell" policy. Since the policy's implementation in 1993, taxpayers have paid more than $230 million to carry out its discriminatory policies. The military claims it must spend millions in advertising to recruit new members, yet it spends millions more discharging hundreds of recruits every year—not because those recruits are doing an inadequate job but simply because of their sexual orientation. This is unacceptable!

American military personnel serve alongside troops from Great Britain, Israel, Canada, the Czech Republic, Sweden, and other countries with policies that do not discriminate against gay and lesbian service members, yet the "don't ask, don't tell" policy remains in place.

Closeted gay and lesbian service personnel are currently deployed in the Middle East, yet if any of them are wounded, they are forbidden from turning to a fellow soldier and requesting, "Please call my partner and let him know I'm OK." Gay and lesbian military personnel cannot have pictures of their partners in their wallets, can't make phone calls home—in short, can't tell anyone *anything* about their personal lives. Even if some personnel live in cities, counties, or states that protect domestic partnerships, they cannot exercise those protections without risking being kicked out of the military.

Is this the best we can do for the men and women who put their lives on the line to defend our country? I think not. Please help to overturn "don't ask, don't tell."

Sincerely,

YOUR NAME AND ADDRESS HERE

Appendix D
Sample Letter to Senator to Overturn the Defense of Marriage Act

The Honorable Frank Lautenberg
324 Hart Senate Building
Washington, DC 20510

Dear Senator Lautenberg:

Please take action to remove the so-called "Defense of Marriage Act," which defines marriage as a "union between a man and a woman" and denies any federal relationship benefits to same-sex couples. There is no rational purpose for this law other than to deny gay, lesbian, and transsexual American citizens the rights afforded opposite-sex married couples. The Defense of Marriage Act is a mean-spirited law that denies same-sex couples the security of the "full faith and credit" clause of the U.S. Constitution and principles of comity, which require states to recognize and enforce marriages performed in other states.

Same-sex couples are currently being denied access to the 1,138 federal rights, benefits, protections, and responsibilities that come with civil marriage, including the right to file income taxes jointly, the right of spouses to receive Social Security benefits, and the right to sponsor an immigrant partner. Civil marriage is a contractual arrangement with both federal and state governments. It's unfair that the government refuses to let American citizens enter into these contracts when our neighbors to the north have realized that denying same-sex couples the right to marry is unconstitutional, as have the High Courts of Vermont, Hawaii, and Massachusetts.

With Canada's full recognition of marriages between two partners of the same sex, litigation pending in New

Jersey, and current legislation in New York, it is likely that same-sex couples will be granted access to civil marriage in the near future, yet stopped short by the DOMA. Please act now to remove this unjust federal law so that same-sex couples who marry in one state will not become legal strangers after crossing the state lines—currently the case for any couple registered in a Vermont civil union. Please protect all families by introducing or cosponsoring legislation to remove what would more accurately be called the "Denial of Marriage Act" from the books.

Sincerely,

YOUR NAME AND ADDRESS HERE

Appendix E
Sample Letter to Senators to Support Domestic Partnership Benefits for Federal Employees

The Honorable George Allen
204 Russell Senate Office Building
Washington, DC 20510

Dear Senator Allen:

Please support the Domestic Partnership Benefits and Obligations Act (DPBO) (S. 1252 and HR 2426) so that lesbian, gay, bisexual, and transsexual federal employees can provide the basic relationship protections of health care and pension benefits to their same-sex partners.

As you know, many federal employees work in dangerous settings to ensure that all Americans obtain the benefits and protections of our government. However, lesbian, gay, bisexual, and transsexual people considering civil service employment must choose between their country and providing basic protections to their loved ones (partners and children). No one should be asked to make this choice. Failing to provide health care and pension benefits to same-sex partners is denying patriotic lesbian, gay, bisexual, and transsexual people the opportunity to serve their country. Unlike their heterosexual coworkers who are able to marry, LGBT people who choose federal employment over corporate or nonprofit work leave their families uncovered by health insurance, or they are forced to pay higher health care costs.

Many Fortune 500 companies are truly committed to a diverse workforce. Ford Motor Company, Wells Fargo, and Charles Schwab all see the importance of providing domestic partners benefits to their employees. Why? Because the policy helps to retain good employees. Because

LGBT people make up only 10% of the population, and many are still single, providing domestic partnership benefits to LGBT federal employees with same-sex partners would be fiscally insignificant.

I urge you to consider the value of LGBT employees and to treat their families fairly by supporting the Federal Domestic Partnership Bill that would allow federal employees access to domestic partnership benefits.

Thank you for honoring diversity and supporting all families.

Sincerely,

YOUR NAME AND ADDRESS HERE

Appendix F
Sample Letter to Senators

The Honorable Senator Barbara Boxer
1700 Montgomery St., Suite 240
San Francisco, CA 94111

Dear Senator Boxer:
Please take a stand for full equality for all Americans.
For far too long, this country, and its elected leaders, have allowed gay, lesbian, bisexual, and transsexual individuals to be treated as second-class citizens. Sadly, our government has waited for such discrimination to be less popular before taking action to end it.

Imagine what the world would have been like if Rosa Parks had waited for it to be "popular" before she refused to give up her bus seat, or if Lyndon B. Johnson had waited for a majority of Americans to be "colorblind" before pushing integration forward. Just how long would it have taken for a majority of American voters to support integration?

Change is never easy. It requires leaders and citizens to step out of their comfort zones and do not what is popular, but what is right. This was the level of commitment shown by white college students who registered black voters in the South and white ministers who went on the Freedom Rides.

As my elected official, please set aside your personal comfort zone and take a leadership role for the **full equality of all Americans** regardless of sexual orientation by pursuing the following paths to justice:

1. Urge the Pentagon to **"lift the ban"** on gays in the military. All Americans should have the choice to protect and serve their country openly.
2. Come out against the Federal Marriage Amendment

because it would destroy thousands of families in domestic partnerships, civil unions, and marriages performed in Canada. Protect our constitution against all enemies, even those who use patriotic propaganda and rhetoric as their pulpit. The Constitution was intended to guarantee and protect rights, not take them away from a minority group that cannot represent itself.

3. Work to repeal the "Denial of Marriage" Act and to secure **marriage equality in all 50 states.** Educate yourself and others on why those 1,138 rights, responsibilities, and protections matter to gay people. Help others understand, as Dr. Martin Luther King, Jr. so clearly did, that "Injustice anywhere is a threat to justice everywhere!"

4. Cosponsor the **Domestic Partnership Benefits and Obligations Act,** which will grant the same benefits, including pension and health insurance coverage, to the domestic partners of federal employees and the **Tax Equity for Health Plan Beneficiaries Act (H.R. 935).**

5. Support the **Permanent Partners Immigration Act** and help others understand the devastating effects on binational same-sex couples fostered by denying American citizens the right to sponsor an immigrant partner.

Your efforts in this fight for equality are greatly appreciated!

Sincerely,

YOUR NAME AND ADDRESS HERE

Acknowledgments

I want to thank the Creator for teaching me how to make lemonade out of lemons.

Thanks to my amazing wife, Molly McKay, for her inspiration in all areas of my life, but especially for being my muse. Her example continues to inspire me to keep preaching the merits of same-sex marriage and equal rights for all people. I thank her for her endless support and enthusiasm in keeping me going on this project and for her editorial efforts in the wee hours of the night before my deadlines. Thank you, Molly. You are my everything!

I also want to thank my phenomenal editor, Terri Fabris, for giving me honest feedback and space to pursue my writing and my neurotic fear of success without judgment. Thanks to Shar Rednour for sharing her connection to Alyson Books and for so generously praising the work Molly and I have done. I also want to thank Erin Fisher, my Landmark Coach, who encouraged me to put pen to paper in the first place. To the best writing teacher I have ever known, Martivon Galindo, thanks for helping me believe that I had something to say and for all your gentle encouragement. I am also grateful for the work done by editorial assistant Whitney Friedlander.

I want to thank all of my friends, especially Kristen Valus, Cary Littel, Tara Zampardi, Lynne Bartz, Robin Beringer, Nikki West, and Stephanie Rosenbaum who supported me with praise, encouragement, and assistance with other projects so I could focus on this one. Thanks to my supportive family Richard Kotulski, Janice Duchon, Louann Kotulski, Ray Parker, Abs Kotulski, Richard W. Kotulski, Barbara Whitman, Chuck Whitman, and Nan, Jim, John, and Heidi McKay. Special thanks to my sister-in-law, Amy Kotulski, for her promotion of this book and for her constant support.

I want to thank NCLR's Kate Kendall, Shannon Minter, Alma Soongi Beck, and Courtney Joslin for helping me present the legal issues; Freedom to Marry's Evan Wolfson for his priceless advice and support; Jon W. Davidson at Lambda Legal for allowing me to reprint the chart on AB205; and the Oakland PFLAG chapter for sharing their satirical version of how we should redefine marriage according to biblical doctrine.

Finally, I want to thank the board members, chapter leaders, and members of Marriage Equality California, who have spent and still spend numerous weekends with clipboards in hand educating people about why they should give a damn about same-sex marriage. Your hard work has made a huge difference in the world, from San Francisco to Pueblo Indian reservations in New Mexico; the backwoods of Lynchburg, Virginia; and the jungles of Peru. The message is being heard: All individuals deserve to be able to marry the person they love.

To all our relations!